THE CUSHION BOOK

The Cushion Book

CREATIVE IDEAS TO MAKE AND DECORATE

Juliet Bawden

Photography by Marie-Louise Avery

NEW HOLLAND

Dedication
For John and Anna French

First Published in the UK in 1995 by
New Holland (Publishers) Ltd
24 Nutford Place, London W1H 6DQ

ISBN 1 85368 524 0 (hbk)
ISBN 1 85368 525 9 (pbk)

Editor: Emma Callery
Designer: Peter Crump
Illustrators: Coral Mula and Julie Ward
Jacket author photograph: Shona Wood

Editorial direction: Yvonne McFarlane

Reproduction by Hirt and Carter,
Cape Town, South Africa

Printed and bound in Hong Kong by
South China Printing Co Ltd

Acknowledgements

The author wishes to thank the
following companies for their
generous help in putting this
book together:

DMC Creative World Ltd,
Pullman Road,
Wigston,
Leicestershire
LE18 2DY
(0533) 811040
*for providing threads and AIDA
materials for the cross stitch
project.*

Elna
*for the use of their sewing
machine*

Creative Beadcraft Ltd
Denmark Works
Sheepcote
Dell Road
Beamond End
Near Amersham
Buckinghamshire
HP7 0RX
*for sequins, beads and metallic
trims used in the embellishment
of cushions*

Philip and Tacey
North Way
Andover
Hampshire
SP10 5BA
*for the marbling kit used in the
marbled cushion*

Harvey Nichols
Knightsbridge
London SW1
Telephone: 0171 235 5000
for the loan of designer cushions

Anna French
343 Kings Road
London SW3 5ES
for the loan of cushions

Cushions
Unit 6
98 Victoria Road
London NW10 6NB
Telephone: 0181 963 0994
for the loan of cushions

George Weil and Sons Ltd
18 Hanson Street
London W1P 7DB
Telephone: 0171 580 3763

Hays Colours Ltd
55/57 Glengall Road
London SE15 6NQ

Philippa Graham
*for the loan of her historic
cushions*

Appletons Yarn
Appleton Bros
Church St
London W4
Telephone: 0181 994 0711
*for yarns in the Needlepoint
Cushion*

Contents

Introduction

Dear reader, if you do not already know, I will let you into a secret — the last section of a book to be written is usually the one that comes first — the introduction. So, after many months of very enjoyable work, I will now tell you about the evolution of this book. When I started writing it, I naïvely wondered if I was going to be able to fill the pages with interesting and diverse styles of cushions. I hope that you will agree that I have managed to do just that.

In fact, the biggest problem has been deciding what to leave out and when to stop. It became so bad, my editor said, 'You have got to stop now, there is no room for any more,' as yet another treasure was discovered. There are so many designers out there creating wonderful cushions and the range in materials and styles is equally vast.

To whet your appetite, the book begins with a gallery full of inspirational cushions in a variety of styles designed to please most tastes. Some cushions are more classic than others, and others are just plain fun, such as the crocheted sunflowers and the felt matryoshka doll, but all are practical.

A whole range of techniques has been used to make and decorate the cushions featured in the main section of this book, and there are some additional exciting embellishing ideas following on. All the projects have clear, step-by-step instructions and photographs (although they do assume a certain level of knowledge, such as being able to work cross stitch or tent stitch for the embroidered cushions) and they are followed by a practical section showing how to make cushions in a variety of styles.

Cushions are more than just a way of decorating a room. Depending on what they are made from, they can add luxury and contrast to a colour scheme. They can add texture, they can make a room cosy or they can be a blank canvas on which to add accent colour or some sort of statement. This need not be complex. We have a whole section (see Embellishments and fastenings on pages (108-17) showing various ways of embellishing existing cushions from the very simple — by the addition of covered buttons — to more complex appliqué, or just by adding piping or different kinds of trimmings.

I hope you enjoy reading and using this book.

Juliet Bawden

$\mathcal{S}$TYLES OF CUSHIONS

Historical overview

The history of furniture has been chronicled since the time of the Egyptian Pharaohs, but it is known that cushions were around long before then. For example, it is believed that pads of fur wrapped around leaves or straw were the first form of furniture. Moving further forwards in time, the Romans had a fondness for luxury and are known to have made their beds and chairs more comfortable with fine coloured stuffs and pillows. However, as with all textiles and soft furnishings, cushions have unfortunately not stood the test of time very well as they are adversely affected by too much light and poor humidity. Made of fabrics that wear out or perish over the years, and stuffed with equally vulnerable materials, only the most treasured examples have survived, and there is not a vast amount of information available on these soft furnishing accessories.

Embroidered cushions

The history of cushions is, of course, directly linked with that of textiles, and one of the most important streams of this must be embroidery. Although the art of embroidery can be traced back for centuries, the oldest attributable piece of English work is dated at around AD 850. Remaining examples of English medieval embroidery are scarce and almost exclusively religious. This does not mean that other embroidery,

such as for clothing and furnishing, was not produced, only that little has survived.

From the Reformation onwards, it is the other way round, however, with most Tudor and Jacobean embroidery being secular. House furnishing became a more important and lucrative market, with a more prosperous and stable society able to spend and vaunt its new-found wealth on luxuries and lavish possessions. Unfortunately, much of the embroidery made of the most expensive materials — such as silver thread and seed pearls — was dismantled in order to be re-used, so again, very few such cushions remain.

More examples exist of the embroidery technique widely used for furnishings where cheaper materials such as silk or wool were stitched all over the base fabric

PREVIOUS PAGE
Four monotone silk-screened cushions in various shades of white, black and grey. A chic finish is achieved by the use of a piped edge made from bias-cut striped cotton.
(Cindy Shear)

BELOW
A Victorian crazy patchwork cushion made from pieces of left-over fabric from the royal dressmaker.
(Loaned by Phillipa Graham)

— often linen or canvas — to cover it entirely. Another method was to embroider on an exposed linen ground. This was popular for decorating tablecloths and pillows, as well as vestments. Inspiration for patterns came from various sources, including printed works. For example, a number of the scenes from Genesis, embroidered on a set of four pillow covers in the Victoria & Albert Museum's collection, are based on H.S. Beham's *Biblicae Historiae*, Frankfurt (1537), and the first scene in the pillow from this set has figures taken from Holbein's *Dance of Death*.

Embroidery on furnishings

One form of embroidery widely used for the coverings of 17th-century seat furniture is 'Irish stitch', or point d'Hongrie, a flame-like, zigzag pattern. Embroidery

throughout the 17th and most of the 18th centuries continued to play a big part in furnishings, with canvas remaining the basic ground material, be it for floor carpets, cushions, or embroidered seats for sets of chairs.

There were some changes though. Fine silk embroidery was largely replaced by crewel wool on heavy linen-cotton twill. For professional use, silk thread was also used widely during the 18th century, sometimes in conjunction with metal thread. Items made included bed sets composed of coverlet, valance, bolster and pillows.

17th-century cushions and upholstery

Cushions had been very much prized among the upper classes during the Middle Ages. Like tapestries, they were movable furniture, and became a status symbol, a declaration of opulence. From a practical point of view, the medieval lord led an unsettled existence, and needed furniture that could be easily moved. Trestle-tables, folding chairs, folding beds, tapestries and cushions were the order of the day.

By the 17th century, however, the upper classes were more settled, even if they did tend to have more than one house or mansion to keep up — a town house and a country house at the very least. Less necessity to move was reflected in the changing fashion of furniture, but a show of opulence was equally important, with many a social and business associate invited into the family home, and proof (or at least semblance) of

a solid financial background therefore became a must.

The 17th-century house was not just a home, it was a status symbol. In view of this, the upholsterer's designs, opinions and contacts were of optimum importance to the final appearance of an important man's house. Luxurious 17th-century bedding would include sheets, blankets — usually of wool or fustian (a hard-wearing mix of cotton and either wool or flax) — quilts, a counterpane, pillows and bolsters.

The pillows and bolsters were usually filled with feathers, and although English beds rarely had more than two pillows, in other European countries it became a sign of rank to have a large number. Some of the more flamboyant of the gentry are said to have had countless cushions of various shapes and sizes, one is even documented as having a pillow on which to rest her thumb! In the Elizabethan era, 'book pillows' were still in use. Often beautifully embroidered, they protected books, which were themselves a luxury, from wear and tear on the binding. In early Stuart times, a cushion played a central part in a lively popular dance known as the cushion dance, the major feature of which was that kissing took place on a cushion.

Developments in the States

During the 17th century in the USA, wealthy colonists had sheets and pillow-cases made of fine linen, but most households used a coarser material such as canvas, holland, or hempen (a cream-coloured, rough linen). However, as elsewhere, fashions in bedding changed with the times. The Victorian ladies' magazine *The Delineator* instructed, 'The pillows are of a required shape, being almost square; while the spread is of bolton [cotton] sheeting, left particularly plain.'

Traditionally, American women marked bed and table linens by embroidering numbers and initials on them. In this way, a woman not only kept track of how many sheets and pillowcases she had made, she could also rotate them by number and prevent uneven wear and tear. As well as her name, she sometimes included a religious motto or a romantic sentiment. Sarah Gordon of Bedford, New Hampshire, had this poem on her pillowcase along with the date (1821):

Sarah, may angels guard thy bed,
And Hover o'er thy pillow'd head,
May heaven, all kind, omnipotent and wise
Appoint some seraph from his blissful skies
To guard thee over with tender care
And of all blessings mayest thou have a
    share.

Most American bedrooms at this time had a variety of pillowcases, usually made from finely bleached linen. Pillowcasings were known as 'pillow-beares', had two to four linen-twill ties at one end and were finished with narrow hems.

Lavish pillow shams were often made to accompany matching spreads. They would be embroidered, candlewicked or made of stuffed work, but by 1850, buttons and buttonholes were in vogue and these

ABOVE
Modern copies of
Victorian flowers and
wreath needlepoint
cushions. Small in scale,
they are pretty and look
just right in their
cottage environment.
(Damask)

RIGHT
A ruby-red velvet
cushion embellished
with an old chenille
rose and edged with old
gold piping.
(Author's collection)

Towards the Arts and Crafts

A lavish use of cushions among the upper classes continued well into the 19th century, with many an early Victorian placing as much of an emphasis on interior comfort and opulence as their predecessors. They delighted in overstuffed cushions covered in velvet and trimmed with fringes, with a seasonal option of loose chintz covers to lighten a room. This trend, however, would shortly disappear, when the influence of the Arts and Crafts movement put an end to the over-exuberance of this flamboyant taste. Frills and flounces became a definite 'no-no' in fashionable society, with upholstery dramatically simplified, and with only occasional use of cushions on chairs and sofas. Window seats were popular though, made more comfortable with box cushions and a few scatter cushions, often covered in contrasting patterned fabrics.

replaced the twill ties. Late Victorian cases were huge and square with fancy edging, scalloping and embroidery.

Between 1830 and 1860, a unique type of pillowcase was developed by Pennsylvanian German women. They were pieced and appliquéd to match quilts of the same design. Usually made in pairs they were used to dress beds for special occasions and were probably only washed twice a year.

Interior decor followed many trends throughout the 18th and 19th centuries. However, the much simpler and sparser fashions (including the Federal style popular in the United States in the late 18th and early 19th centuries) had little use for the effect of pomp and luxury which cushions can give to a room. Private individuals exercised greater choice, though, and so it was that Benjamin Franklin provided his wife with two different prints for drapes and chairs, 'Because these were my fancy'.

Pincushions

With a miniature history all of their own, the legacy of pincushions reveals a labour of love and care in attention to detail which defy the constricting proportions of these endearing little cushions. Pins were originally made of thorns or bones, and as they were delicate enough to need protecting they were kept wrapped in skin. Later pins would have been kept in small boxes or cylindrical cases and so pincushions as we know them, or pin-pillows, came into being around the end of the 16th century.

Often lavishly embroidered, pincushions became essential accessories through many a changing fad. During the 17th century, embroidered draw-string purses usually had a small matching pincushion hanging from the main body by a cord. A pincushion would also be found in the 17th-century boudoir, and could be mounted in silver to match a dressing table set.

By the 18th century, pincushions were mounted on box lids, and hanging pincushions also became popular around about this time. They could be inscribed with political, historical or amorous messages, sometimes worn hanging from garters!

Impractical but aesthetically pleasing were pin-stuck cushions, decorated with elaborate patterns of pins or beads attached with pins.

Church kneelers

A sub-culture of cushion craft exists in the form of embroidered church kneelers. Many of these have been designed and worked by groups of local people, to a greater or lesser degree of aesthetic success, but always with skill and dedication. These craftspeople have drawn inspiration for designs from all around, be it the architecture of the church itself, the colours and motifs of the stained-glass windows, religious themes, motifs inspired by nature, or even the more unusual and offbeat (examples include the Arc de Triomphe and a Chinese panda!).

Although it seems natural to assume that the history of embroidered church kneelers can be traced back at least a few centuries, most are, in fact, less than half a century old — the first documented project of furnishing a church with kneelers was in 1929.

Cushions around the world

It is pretty safe to assume that any textile craft which has ever been popular has also been used in the making of cushions, be it

LEFT
Nineteenth-century kelims do not always survive intact. They are often cut up and made into cushions such as those on the left. *(Loaned by Philippa Graham)*

RIGHT
A collection of
nineteenth-century
Indian cushions made
out of old embroidered,
appliquéd and mirrored
fabrics.
*(Loaned by Liz
Mundel)*

FAR RIGHT
An example of finely
woven pre-First World
War sari fabric recycled
to make a cushion.

weaving, tapestry, patchwork, batik or whatever. Unfortunately, many historical and ethnic textile and craft books tend to concentrate more on other soft furnishing objects such as rugs and quilts, or on clothing such as throws and shawls. Nevertheless, these are a wonderful source of reference for techniques, and also for inspiration and ideas for patterns and colours to be used in cushion design.

Books on quilting and patchwork by American settlers, and painted fabric and appliqué by native Americans, are breathtaking references to traditional, but often surprisingly refreshing, textile designs.

Batik still thrives in Indonesia, a tradition being kept very much alive and well worth experimenting with, as the resulting effects are always unique. Similarly, Indian textiles are as colourful, breathtaking, varied and surprising as the culture itself. Ideas include beautiful, bright animal figures appliquéd onto cushions for children, embroidering bold simple designs in thick colourful yarns, and hand-dyeing cheap fabrics for subtle and unusual colourways.

The same applies across the five continents, with traditional Australian Aboriginal, African and South American techniques and designs being just three other possible starting points! It is interesting to compare different cultural designs — their apparent simplicity or eccentricity often disguises a very sophisticated use of colour and form — to see how ideas have evolved and influenced other generations.

If all these new techniques sound a little daunting, then attractive, ethnic-style cushions can be made very simply by using ready-made textiles from around the world, or by sewing interesting pieces onto a backing, or even mix-and-matching them — all very useful ways of using up pieces of fabric too small for any other use.

Gallery

Cushions come in numerous shapes and sizes and can be made from a variety of fabrics and fillings. Bolsters, squabs and pillows may all be described as cushions, but they each have different uses. For example, a bolster may be used as an arm rest or a head rest. A cushion on a window seat makes a wooden perch into somewhere comfortable to sit. Almost all wicker furniture looks better with the addition of cushions or squabs, and most chairs and sofas benefit from cushions as they immediately appear more comfortable when heaped with cushions.

Just as jewellery, handbag and shoes can tone with or add contrast to an outfit, so cushions add a style accent to a room, for they are its accessories. The following pages show how cushions can bring colour accents to a room or create particular styles. For example, clean, crisp colours in unfussy fabrics may generate a rather masculine effect (see pages 34-5). This can be created by using a limited colour palette, such as in the work of Sarah King, aided by appliquéing more traditional patterns onto a modern fabric to create new and exciting designs.

Cushions do not necessarily have to be made of woven fabric or be symmetrical in design. Hikaru Noguchi makes her cushions from wool, for example, and the one on page 21 uniquely looks like a nest.

Outdoor cushions need to be taken in during damp weather, but they may take their inspiration from nature. The batik cushions on page 23, with their splashes of red, are the very colours to be seen in early autumn. These batik cushions are also made in summer colours with fish and animal imagery. Cushions are great for conservatory and summer house use, where they make the transition from indoor to outdoor living a little more comfortable.

As well as for use in sitting rooms and lounges, cushions have their place in the dining room. If there are children around they should be made in washable fabrics, with pads separate from the cover. They may be attached to dining room chairs or placed on a window seat or even serve as floor cushions in an odd corner.

Children's bedrooms can be decorated with cushions in primaries, sugared almond or baby soft colours (see pages 30-1). Embroidery, cross stitch or appliqué are all good ways of decorating baby cushions. It is very important that everything is sewn on well so that nothing may be swallowed accidentally.

Bedroom cushions (see pages 32-3) should be elegant, large, square, French style, and made from crisp broderie anglaise, which looks wonderful on an old-fashioned bed. Or how about toile de Jouy cushions, which, on a coverlet of the same design, can look warm and welcoming? These are just a few suggestions — there are many other styles and ideas covered in the next section of this book.

LEFT
A collection of cushions made from a variety of techniques and embellishments including Hawaiian appliqué, silk screen printing, covered buttons, star sequins, felt appliqué and hand painting.
Metallic and dressing gown cord, and lampshade fringing, may all be used to edge cushions.

Scatter cushions

Create an irresistibly inviting atmosphere with mounds of cushions heaped onto a favourite chair or sofa. Use scatter cushions to pick up colour details in the upholstery or curtains, either contrasting or coordinating with your colour scheme. Use them to bring separate elements together, such as a blue from a vase or jug and the yellow from the wallpaper. In this way you can successfully cooordinate the colours in a room. Or if your room is very light and needs some contrast, use a different shade of the wall or floor covering or a strong opposite colour.

ABOVE
Silk cushions made in a variety of subtle colours and stripes. Some are edged with piping, others are left plain. The use of neutral colours makes these cushions very flexible as a design accessory; they can be used in a variety of settings and colour schemes.
(*The Mulberry Tree*)

LEFT
Scatter cushions made from silk in intense reds and blues that look almost velvet-like in their quality.
(*Clare Cox*)

RIGHT
A collection of pretty, traditional-style cushions suitable for a sitting room or bedroom. There is a chambray cushion with a sampler-style alphabet worked in white embroidery; a flower appliqué design in small print, soft-coloured, toning fabrics; a folk-style cushion worked in chain stitch; a toile de Jouy cushion with a pretty pleated frill, and a calico cushion with an overlay of ticking and contrasting running stitch.

Shaped cushions

Cushions come in many shapes and sizes. On these two pages there are examples of heart-, wedge-, cube-, and completely nebulous-shaped cushions. The addition of a frill, border or fringe can change the shape of a cushion and its apparent size. Often cushions are specially shaped to give comfort to a certain part of the body, for example a neck cushion is made to support the head. Shaped cushions may be made to fit an odd corner such as the fireside seat in the picture below.

LEFT
An interesting corner and a visual feast has been created in this fireside seat, using a bolster with a contrasting black and white pompon fringe, two heart-shaped cushions and a foot stool, all made from silk-screened and hand-coloured silk. The imagery is very modern and the colours used are often vibrant.
(Zara Siddiqui)

RIGHT
These shaped cushions are just right for a child's room. As they are shaped like dice they are fun to look at, and they are child-like in scale and light so they may be hurled around without causing damage. The squab cushions are useful for seating small persons on adult-sized chairs.
(Anna French)

LEFT
A wonderful woolly cushion becomes a talking point with its nest-like appearance. It feels extraordinarily comfortable as a cushion but works equally well as a nest for some lemons and a yellow chick.
(Hikaru Noguchi)

Bolsters

Bolsters are normally seen at either end of a sofa, chaise-longue or day bed, and as they were used more for support than comfort, they are usually firm. Traditionally, bolsters are covered in a white linen case and stretched from one side of a bed to the other. They may be finished in a variety of ways, including tassels, frills or piped ends with covered buttons. The choice of fabric for your bolster depends on where it is to be used. Choose machine-washable fabrics for bedroom use and hardwearing fabrics for sitting rooms.

ABOVE
A very pretty toile de Jouy print in pink on a cream base is used to create a bolster for a bedroom. The pleated edge and self-made tie add to the femininity of the design.
(Damask)

LEFT
Large-scale, masculine bolsters based on a nautical theme, these cushions are made from canvas with a flat placket opening punched with eyelets through which is threaded rope.
(Hampshire and Dillon)

RIGHT
Two bolsters made
from batik fabric which
is then cut into
patchwork, rearranged
and sewn into bolsters.
The imagery is taken
from nature — leaves,
shells and stones, with
the colours of autumn
being predominant.
(Alison Tilley)

Conservatories

Unless you are lucky enough to live in a perfect climate, conservatories can be inhospitable to fabrics. The sun will bleach colours and the damp may rot them. So choose fabric with care and have a dry place to store the cushions when necessary. Cushions made with waterproof bases are ideal for outdoor living as they will not be damaged when you sit on the floor. Wicker furniture is often used in a conservatory, but it is hard and cushions will make it more comfortable.

OPPOSITE
Natural forms such as fish, chickens, parrots and the flow of water are the inspiration behind these silk batik cushions. A textured appearance is achieved by applying the wax using a sponge. They are ideal for a garden room or conservatory.
(Roz Arno)

LEFT
These hardwood chairs bought from Africa after the Second World War need cushions with a bold design that will not be lost by the size of the chairs on which they are placed. These cushions have been made by appliquéing simple shapes onto an old blanket.
(Lisa Vaughan)

OVERLEAF LEFT
Three hand-stencilled cushions feature traditional motifs of fleur-de-lys, grids and vine leaves. They have been given a modern treatment by using a subtle colour palette of luxurious rich, warm colours.
(Bery Designs)

OVERLEAF RIGHT
These cushions from the same interiors collection show how simple geometric shapes can take on a depth and subtlety by applying layers of coloured texture to break up the surface.
(Anna French)

Painted silk

Stretched silk may be painted onto directly, using a gutta outliner and ink paints that are fixed by steaming or ironing on the back of the fabric. Acid dyes may also be used to decorate fabrics by hand painting or silk screen printing and the fabric can then be turned into cushions. Always choose the best silk possible for making cushions, as thin silk will pull and distort easily unless backed with a more sturdy fabric. The silk cushions shown right are very bright, but silk paints are also available in light and soft tones.

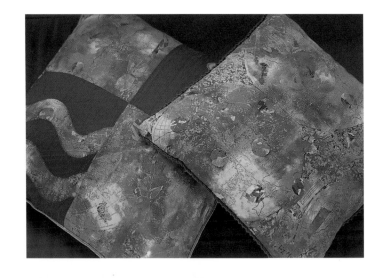

ABOVE
The cushions above are created by making collages from home-produced and dyed felt. The design is then photographed and copied onto a silk screen. When the fabric is printed, the designer cuts it into pieces and creates a further collage.
(*Liz Mundle*)

LEFT
These large floor cushions are printed using discharge dyes to bleach out the background colour.
(*Dawn Dupree*)

Realistic sunflowers, vegetables and plates of food worked in vibrant colours create a trompe-l'oeil effect on these large, luxurious cushions. A strong design statement such as this is not for the faint hearted. When choosing bold colours and images such as these, it is important to go overboard both in colours and quantity of cushions.
(Kim Meyer)

Bedrooms for children

In the past, children's rooms were always decorated either in pastel or primary colours and this included accessories such as cushions. Designers who produced adult ranges tended to ignore children. Happily, times have changed as the lovely designs shown here from Anna French and Damask show. Children are messy creatures, so it is a good idea to make sure any cushion for a child's room is machine washable. Also, when making children's cushions be sure that the cushions are small enough in scale to fit the child's furniture and that everything is well sewn so there is no danger of a child swallowing any embellishment or button.

BELOW
Ships are the theme of this cushion, but instead of the usual child's depiction of a yacht, it is a nineteenth century steamer. Here is a cushion that sits as easily on a small cane seat chair used as a nursing chair as it does on a child's bed or seat.
(*Anna French*)

OPPOSITE
Although childlike in concept, these Oxford cushions are sophisticated in design with a stripy tiger, a teddy in his nautically striped tee-shirt and a tiger wearing his own stripes. These are all enchanting nursery cushions.
(*Anna French*)

ABOVE
This cushion is suitable for a baby or a younger child. Machine embroidery has been used to create a sampler-style cushion complete with alphabet and old-fashioned nursery toys, including a doll, teddy, hobby horse and beach ball.
(*Damask*)

Feminine bedrooms

The term feminine bedroom conjures up a variety of images from the soft and frilly in pastel colours to clean and crisp white linen with or without lace. Toiles de Jouy fabrics with their rustic scenes of everyday life, pastoral landscapes, ancient buildings, classical figures and motifs are perfect for an understated European look. Or a more seductive bedroom would be one with a bed stacked with satin cushions. The cushions can range from small decorative ones to large bolsters to rest against when sitting up to read. The large square pillows so beloved of the French can be used as both cushion and pillow.

ABOVE
Broderie anglaise and lace cushions produce a decidedly feminine ambience. Lace can be applied to the front of a cushion or it can be made up in panels.

LEFT
Large square pillows/cushions are popular in many continental countries such as France, Germany and Switzerland. Made of linen and cotton, they often do up at the back with flat linen buttons. They need particular care with laundering to keep them sparkling white and pressed.

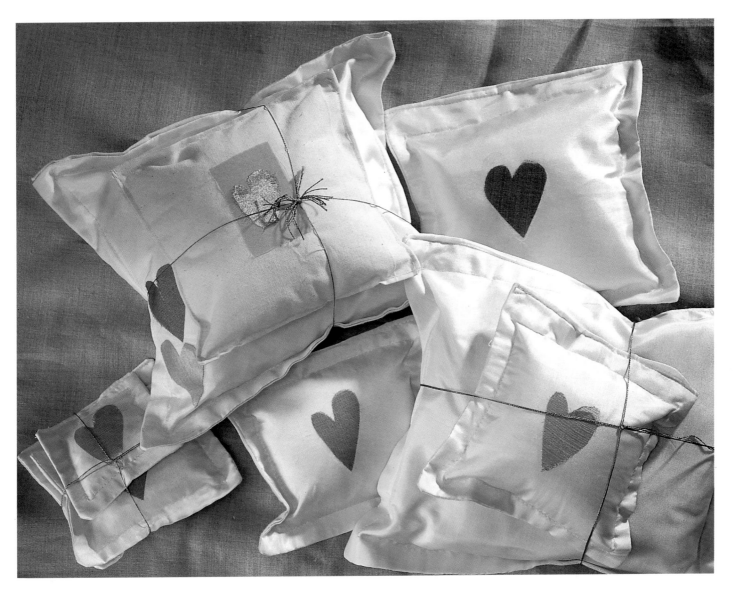

ABOVE
Here is a collection of silk cushions onto
which calico squares and silk hearts have
been bonded using webbing and a hot iron.
The cushions are small and filled with herbs
and pot-pourri. They are excellent for
keeping clothes smelling fresh.
(Rachel McDonnell)

Masculine bedrooms

Masculine bedrooms are frequently bold and simple in design. But because of their soft, giving nature, cushions are usually perceived as female and so it is important to make a strong distinction between male and female cushion styles. Stripes in plain bold colours, or traditional fabrics such as ticking, tartan, towelling and linen (both bleached and unbleached), would not look out of place in a masculine bedroom. Embellishments on masculine cushions should be bold and include piping, cord, tassels and Oxford edges. Buttons and eyelets look better large and motifs are certainly not frilly.

RIGHT
Here the designer has
managed to make a
curvaceous motif look
masculine by the clever
juxtaposition of fabrics,
colours and textures.
The neutral, natural
coloured linen is a
wonderful contrast to
the smooth black
appliquéd design on
its surface.
(Sarah King)

OPPOSITE
Here are three cushions
with bold printed
motifs: a beetle, a shell
and a sun. The edging
detail on these cushions
is bold and unusual
with channels of fabric
broken up to reveal the
cord that passes
through them.
(Hampshire and Dillon)

ABOVE
This cushion is inspired by
antiquity with its marble-like bust
on which is sitting a rather
mischievous cherub. The subtlety
and soft edges of this print make it
a good contrast to the rich, highly
polished chair it is resting upon.
(*Harvey Nichols designer
collection*)

RIGHT
The inspiration for this collection
comes from many sources —
African dancers, Greek pots,
Trojan horses and exotic birds.
The use of a black print on white
cotton pulls together what
otherwise might not read well
together as a collection.
(*Sarah Collins*)

Embroidered cushions

The cushions shown on the next few pages are a mixture of bonded and reverse appliqué, machine embroidery, constructed fabric and machine-knitted cushions. As is apparent from the range of styles shown here, embroidery can be done in many different ways. It can be as simple as a monogram on the corner of a cushion, to the intricacies of layering fabrics one upon another to create a stained-glass effect (like the cushions of Lorna Moffat, seen overleaf). Embroidery may be used to make a figurative statement such as the sun on the cushion opposite or an abstract design such as in the work of Charlotte Hirst.

BELOW
Three velvet cushions decorated with bonded appliqué and gold piping with a gold fringe. Each cushion uses ivy leaves as its theme and yet the pattern on each is inspired and original.
(Sarah King)

ABOVE
These cushions are created from sumptuous fabrics appliquéd and machine embroidered one upon another. The rich palette of colours feature burgundy, deep purple and magenta, with flashes of gold.
(*Charlotte Hirst*)

ABOVE RIGHT
The motif on this cushion is a sun inspired by ancient nautical charts. The work is partly appliquéd and partly machine embroidered, with rich contrasting fabrics to the dark velvet background.
(*Peter Keay*)

RIGHT
This cushion is sewn together to make a patchwork effect.
(*Hikaru Noguchi*)

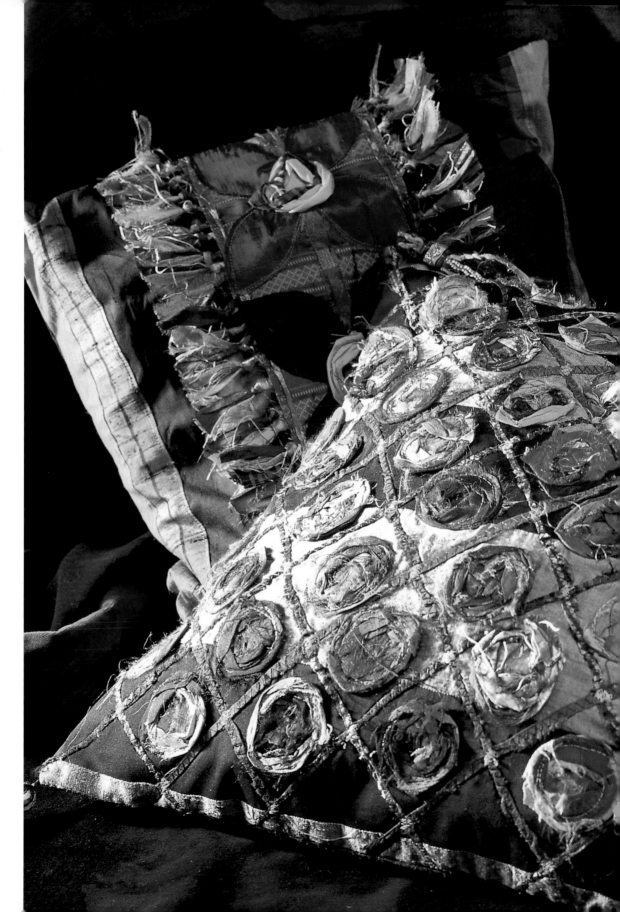

RIGHT
Iridescent organdies
and silks are layered
one upon another, often
as many as six layers.
The design is machine
stitched over all the
layers and then, using
very sharp embroidery
scissors, areas are cut
away to reveal the
layers and colours
below.
(Lorna Moffat)

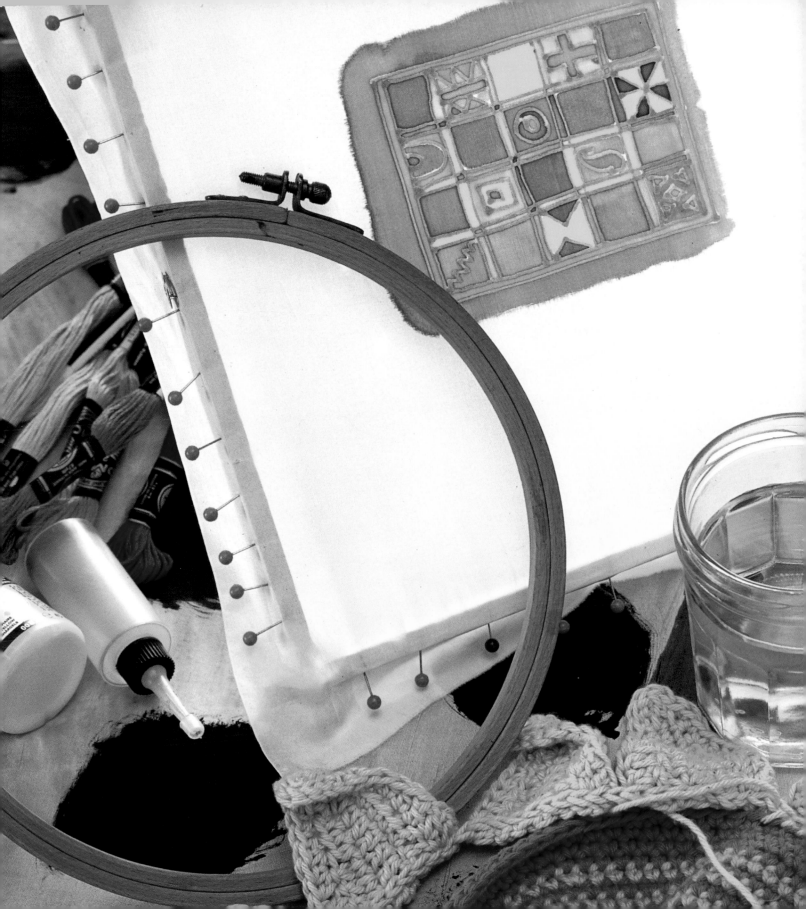

CREATING CUSHIONS

PAINTED CUSHIONS

Cushions may be hand-painted, silk-screen-printed, block-printed, batiked or silk-painted as a means of decoration and each of these processes may be done in one or many colours. The painting may be used to coordinate a cushion with the rest of the furnishings in a room or even to pull together inharmonious colours. The use of colour and the richness of a pattern can change the whole appearance of a piece of cloth. For example, the humble ticking cushion opposite looks sophisticated with its stencilled border design.

The large freehand painted dots and bold splashes of colour on the cushion behind give a bolder statement and altogether more modern style. The detail of the hand-painted silk cushion above shows a richness and subtlety of colour that offers an entirely different ambience.

Stencilled cushions

Stencilling is a very easy technique which if done properly can result in a sophisticated finish. The secret of a good stencil is to have lots of bridges between the different elements of the design. When stencilling, apply a little colour at a time with a dry brush. This will prevent smudging. For depth of colour, start with a little on the brush and add more as you work into the design. These cushions have been designed to coordinate with an antique Paisley shawl made in a bought fabric, which is no longer obtainable. Both the vine leaf motif and the striped fabric echo the colour and pattern of the chair cushion. Inspired by pre-Egyptian Coptic art, this motif was taken from an artifact found at the Victoria and Albert Museum in London.

(DESIGNER: LUCINDA GANDERTON)

MATERIALS & EQUIPMENT

....

carbon paper

stencil card

pencil

tracing paper

cutting mat

craft knife

0.5 m (½ yd) calico or
heavyweight muslin

iron and ironing board

kitchen paper towels

scissors

fabric paints

2 stencil brushes

0.5 m (½ yd) ticking or
striped fabric

cotton threads

sewing machine

61 cm diameter × 45 cm long
(24 × 18 in) bolster pad

2 large 5 cm (2 in) diameter old
coat buttons

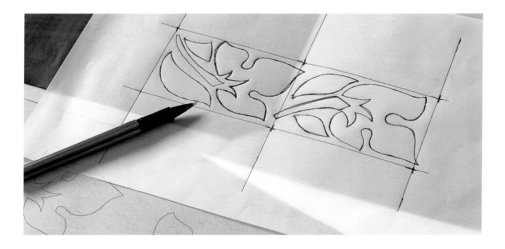

1 Enlarge the design on page 48 on a photocopier to an appropriate size. Place the carbon paper face down on the stencil card and put the photocopied design on top. Trace the flowers onto one sheet of card and the leaves onto another. Do not forget to put clear registration marks in the corners of each of the designs, so you can make quite sure you place the second sheet in the correct place for printing.

OPPOSITE
The same stencil has been used on two edges of a square cushion in a different colourway. The dark red stripe is similar to the colour used for the stencil, so a harmonious composition is formed.

2 *Place the flower design onto the cutting mat and, using a very sharp craft knife, cut away the areas where the colour is going to be applied and the registration marks. Repeat this with the other sheet of stencil paper featuring the leaves.*

Stencil template

3 *Cut two strips of calico or heavyweight muslin each 10 × 60 cm (4 × 24 in) and iron ready for printing. Place the strips onto kitchen paper towels to absorb any excess paint. Mark the registration marks with a pencil for the positioning of the stencil. Pour the fabric paint into a saucer and dip a stencil brush into it. Stamp off any surplus paint onto a* *piece of paper and then stencil the leaves onto the calico strips. Hold the stencil down with one hand and with the other dab the brush vertically up and down until the colour is transferred to the cloth. When no more colour comes from the brush, dip it into the paint again. Dab off the surplus paint before beginning to stencil yet again. Leave to dry.*

LEFT
The flower and leaf stencil outline. Enlarge
to an appropriate size (see step 1).

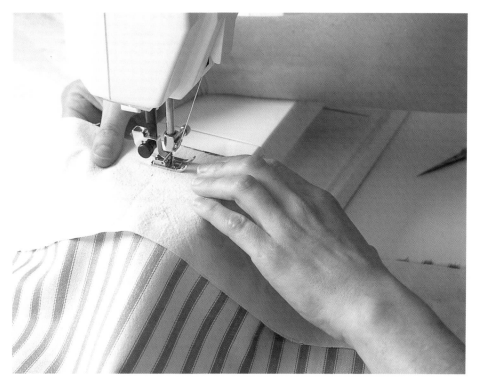

4   *When the first part of the design is dry, making sure the registration marks are in the correct place, and using the other stencil brush, stencil the leaves in a different colour.*

6   *Cut two pieces of striped fabric 20 × 60 cm (8 × 24 in) and cut one piece 25 × 60 cm (10 × 24 in). Using a 1.5 cm (⅝ in) seam allowance, sew a stencilled strip to either side of the wide striped piece of fabric, with right sides facing. Then sew a narrow piece of striped fabric to the outside edges of the stencilled pieces, with right sides facing. Press all the seams flat and then, again with right sides facing, join the long sides to form a tube.*

5   *Using the same stencil brush, stencil a mixture of the two colours onto two large circles of calico which are 10 cm (4 in) in diameter. Leave to dry. They will be used to cover the buttons at the ends of the bolster. Iron all the stencilled pieces of fabric on the back to fix them.*

See also: ◆◆◆◆◆◆◆◆◆◆◆◆

GALLERY p 26
FASTENINGS p 113
PRACTICALITIES pp 123-4, 125

◆◆◆◆◆◆◆◆◆◆◆◆◆◆◆◆◆◆◆◆

7 *Push the bolster pad into the fabric tube, and run a gathering thread 10 cm (4 in) in from the outside edge using large running stitches. Draw up the ends and tuck in the raw edges.*

8 *Cut out the stippled calico circles and again run a gathering thread around each outside edge. Draw up over the button and sew onto the ends of the bolster.*

OPPOSITE
Detail of the cushion end neatly gathered with all the loose ends covered by a button. Note how the shape reflects that of the chair and that the cushion comfortably rests next to the arm.

Silk-painted cushions

Silk painting is becoming very popular as a method of decorating cloth and here it is used to make a gloriously bright cushion. First, barriers of gutta are painted on, much as the lead in a stained-glass window, then the colour is added. It stops at the line of the gutta. Before stretching out the silk, prepare your design, which you will then need to copy onto the fabric. To avoid smudging the paint, it is best to start at the top of the design and work your way down to the bottom. Small mistakes may be rectified by using a cotton bud dipped in water. Also, keep a tissue to hand to mop up any excess paint from your brush.

(DESIGNER: SARBJIT NATT)

MATERIALS & EQUIPMENT
....

iron and ironing board

two 51 cm (20 in) squares
heavy-weight habotai silk

wooden silk frame

three-pronged silk pins or
fine thumb tacks

vanishing textile marker

metallic gutta and applicator

silk paints (various colours)

paintbrushes

paper

sewing machine

zip

45 cm (18 in) square cushion pad

1 *Cut the silk into two even pieces and then wash, dry and press it. Stretch it onto the wooden frame and hold in position with the pins. The fabric must be absolutely taut with no wrinkles.*

OPPOSITE
The finished cushion with its three bold paisley designs in a modern interpretation for the 1990s.

2 *Use the vanishing textile marker to copy your design onto the stretched silk. Vanishing textile markers fade in time, which means that when the work is complete any pen marks still showing will eventually disappear.*

3 *Apply the metallic gutta to the outline of the design. The gutta blocks the mesh of the silk preventing the silk paint bleeding and merging. Allow the gutta to dry thoroughly, which will take about 2 hours. The process can be speeded up considerably with a hair dryer.*

*4 Arrange all the painting
equipment so it is within easy
reach. Then apply the silk paints,
taking care not to splash them or to
go over any of the gutta lines.*

See also: ◆◆◆◆◆◆◆◆◆◆◆◆◆◆

GALLERY pp 20, 28-9
HAND-PAINTED CUSHIONS pp 58-61
PRACTICALITIES pp 120, 125
◆◆◆◆◆◆◆◆◆◆◆◆◆◆◆◆◆◆◆◆◆

5 Paint the central pattern and finally paint a plain border that is 2.5 cm (1 in) wide all around the design. Allow the fabric to dry before removing it from the frame. Then place the painted silk face down between two sheets of clean white paper and iron it according to the manufacturer's instructions to fix the paint. Decorate a second piece of silk as you did the first. With right sides facing sew the two pieces of silk around three sides and then insert a zip into the fourth. Turn right sides out, press and insert the cushion pad.

OPPOSITE
Two further examples
of silk-painted cushions
with piped edges. The
gold gutta outliner
plays a prominent part
in the overall design.

Hand-painted cushions

Most hand-painted textiles tend to be less bold than the cushion shown here. But by using large brushes and bold brush strokes you can make a very strong design statement. Trisha Needham uses hand painting combined with silk screen printing to make one-off designs on scarves, shawls and ties. She has created this cushion design especially for this book.

(DESIGNER: TRISHA NEEDHAM)

OPPOSITE
Bold lines carried out with conviction make this a strong design, which would look good in a modern interior, especially with a neutral colour scheme.

MATERIALS & EQUIPMENT

two 51 cm (20 in) squares silk or pure wool

newspaper

masking tape

tailor's chalk or a soft pencil

dyes mixed with binder, or ready-prepared fabric paints

jam jars

paintbrushes

iron and ironing board

45 cm (18 in) square cushion pad

1 Draw your design onto paper or copy the one opposite. Either fill in with paints or pens or indicate which colours are used where: be as bold as you like. Wash out any finish from the silk or wool and then iron it flat. Cover your worksurface with newspaper and then tape one of the silk squares onto it so that the silk is taut and cannot move. Using either tailor's chalk or a soft pencil, draw the outline of the design onto the silk.

See also: ◆◆◆◆◆◆◆◆◆◆◆◆

GALLERY pp 20, 27-9
SILK-PAINTED CUSHIONS pp 52-7
PRACTICALITIES pp 120, 125
◆◆◆◆◆◆◆◆◆◆◆◆◆◆◆◆◆◆◆◆

2 *Pour some of the first colour into a jam jar and then paint it on using bold brush strokes.*

3 *Change colours and brushes to make lines of different widths.*

4 *Use a large, circular brush to make filled-in circles.*

5 *Then add tonal contrasts with a smaller paintbrush and slightly darker coloured paints. When the paint is dry, remove the masking tape and lift up the cloth. Fix the paints by ironing on the back of the fabric. Repeat steps 1 to 5 on the other silk or wool square.*

6 *To make into a cushion, sew the pieces of fabric together with right sides facing. Stitch around three sides, turn right sides out and press. Insert the cushion pad and sew up the opening on the fourth side.*

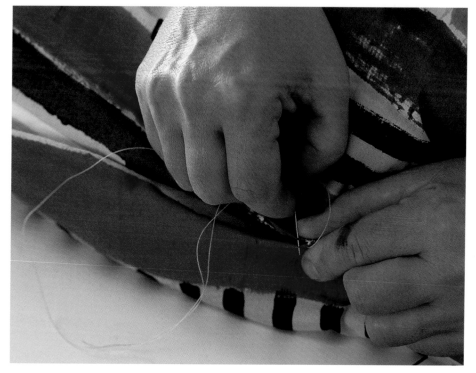

Batik cushions

This style of batik is unusual for instead of dipping the fabric in a dye bath, both the dye and the wax are painted onto the fabric. The end-result is less random than dip dying. When creating her fresh and delicate cushion designs, Alison Tilley is inspired by the patterns, colours and textures of nature, including flowers, leaves, shells and marble.

When using dyes and chemicals, always work in a well-ventilated room and wear protective gloves and a mask.

(DESIGNER: ALISON TILLEY)

To make chemical water
1 Dissolve 4-5 g water softener and 140 g urea in 500 ml (1 pt) hot water.
2 Add cold water to make up 1 litre (2 pt) and store in the plastic water bottle.

To make the dyes
1 Mix 1 ml - 10 ml (¼ tsp - 2 tsp) of each dye powder with a little warm water in an old plastic container to form a paste.
2 Add 100 ml (½ cup) of cold chemical water, according to colour and strength desired.
3 Dissolve 5 ml (1 tsp) of sodium bicarbonate in a little warm water and add to the dye mixture just before use.

OPPOSITE
Batik cushion carried out with the aid of a cardboard stencil. In this method of batik, the wax is applied to the cloth using a paintbrush.

1 Wash the fabric in hot, soapy water to remove impurities which might affect the dye absorption. Dry and iron the fabric and secure it onto your work surface with masking tape. Make the stencil using the outline on page 66 and following the instructions on page 47. Transfer the design onto the cloth with the pencil, and then remove the cloth from the table and stretch it across the wooden frame and attach with thumb tacks.

outline on page 66 and following the instructions on page 47.

MATERIALS & EQUIPMENT

rubber gloves
protective face mask
water softener
urea
1 litre (2 pt) plastic water bottle
cold water fibre reactive dyes
old plastic containers
chemical water
sodium bicarbonate
55 cm (21½ in) square cotton lawn
iron and ironing board
masking tape
carbon paper
stencil card
pencil and tracing paper
cutting mat
craft knife
55 cm (21½ in) wooden frame
thumb tacks
newspaper
foam dye applicator
kitchen paper towels
small heavy saucepan
batik wax granules
electric ring
paintbrush (stiff)
scissors
45 cm (18 in) square cushion pad
cotton thread
sewing machine
55 cm (21½ in) square backing fabric

2 Cover the work surface with newspaper and mix up the first pot (the lightest colour) of dye, as described on the previous page. Using the foam applicator, apply the dye in long even strokes all over the fabric. Should you want to create a mottled effect, sprinkle other colours on while the dye is still wet. Absorb any excess dye with kitchen paper towels and leave to dry thoroughly.

3 Half fill the heavy saucepan with wax granules and heat to a constant temperature of 58°C (136°F). If the wax begins to bubble or smoke it is too hot and needs to be removed from the heat for a while. Remember wax is flammable – never leave unattended. The wax is ready to use when it is transparent. Dip the stiff paintbrush into the wax and paint over the areas of the cloth which you wish to be saved when you apply the next layer of dye. Recharge the brush regularly so the wax fully penetrates the cloth and catch any drips with a piece of kitchen paper towel.

4 *Leave the wax to cool and stiffen. Mix up the second, slightly darker, coloured dye and then paint it on. You will find the areas that you have painted with wax will resist the dye. (Soak up any excess dye with kitchen paper towels.) Leave to dry thoroughly.*

5 *Continue to build up the design by adding alternate layers of wax resist and progressively darker dyes. To finish, cover the whole surface in molten wax and leave to cool. Then take the cloth off the frame and screw into a ball to crack the wax. Re-stretch it on the frame and paint on the final dye, which will seep into the cracks to produce crisp lines of colour. Absorb the excess dye with kitchen paper towels and leave the fabric to air-dry for at least 12 hours.*

See also:

GALLERY pp 23, 25
STENCILLED CUSHIONS pp 48-51
PRACTICALITIES pp 120, 125

6 Remove the wax by ironing the fabric between layers of newspaper. Keep replacing with saturated paper until all absorbed. Dry clean the cloth to remove the last of the wax and finish by washing it in warm soapy water — this is essential to remove the chemicals and excess dye. Rinse in cold running water until clear. Make up the cushion cover by cutting the batik to the same size as the cushion pad plus 12 mm (½ in) seam allowances on each side. Cut the backing fabric to the same size and then make up as on page 61.

Flower outlines

LEFT
Detail showing bright white daisies against a muted greeny-orange background.

RIGHT
The daisy stencil outline. Enlarge to an appropriate size as described on page 47.

RIGHT
Batik cushion made
up of patches. The
border is very light
while the central panel
picks up the bright reds
that often appear in
early autumn.
(Alison Tilley)

Marbled cushions

For this project we have bought pale-coloured plain silk cushions available from good department stores and then removed the covers to marble them with some really vibrant colours. You can, of course, marble onto plain silk fabric and make it up into a cushion if you prefer (see pages 120-5). For a note of luxury we have added brightly coloured silk tassels to the corners, but you needn't stop here. Perhaps you might decide to add bright cording or piping, too — see page 120. For the marbling bath you will find that a photographic developing tray is good for the job if you haven't got anything better. A marbling kit consists of a thickener as well as marbling colours. This is an ideal project for someone who doesn't have a great deal of artistic ability but does have a good eye for colour.

(DESIGNER: JACK MOXLEY)

MATERIALS & EQUIPMENT

marbling kit consisting of thickener and marbling colours
1 litre (2 pt) distilled water
marbling bath
silk cushion cover, washed and dried
iron and ironing board
eye dropper
paintbrush
needle
cotton thread
tassels (brightly coloured)
cushion pad (to fit cover)

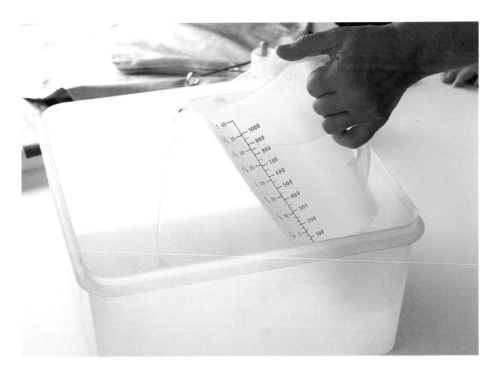

1 *To make the size, mix one heaped teaspoon of the thickening powder with the distilled water and leave to stand for at least an hour so that it turns into a jelly-like substance. Pour the resulting mixture into the marbling bath to a depth of 4-5 cm (1½ to 2 in).*

FACING PAGE
The wonder of marbling on silk is that it is almost random. The rich colours set off by these Eastern silk tassels make them perfect for certain kinds of boudoirs!

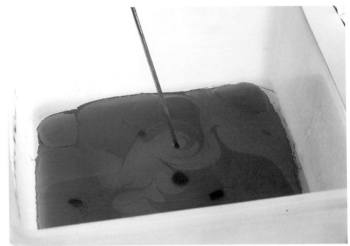

2 Iron the cushion cover with a cool iron. Then, using the eye dropper or a pipette, drop the chosen marbling colours onto the surface of the size. The colours will float on the surface and spread slowly out from the centre of the dropped paint. If you drop too much colour, it will sink to the bottom of the size.

3 When the surface is full of colour make patterns by swirling the paint around with a paintbrush.

4 Very gently lay the cover on top of the medium so that the centre of the cloth touches it first. Let the edges fall into place. Do not move or press the fabric or the pattern will be disturbed. Most fabric becomes translucent when wet so you should be able to see any areas where the pattern has not taken. If this happens, very gently touch the back of the cloth so it makes contact with the medium.

5 *Lift the cover off the gel vertically so that the pattern is not disturbed. Leave to dry and then turn inside out and iron on the back of the cover to fix the design. Turn right sides out and sew the tassels onto each corner and insert the cushion pad.*

RIGHT
Details of the marbled pattern as it sits on the surface of the medium. By stirring the gel with a stick or comb, the pattern can be altered. More colours may be added at this stage if desired.

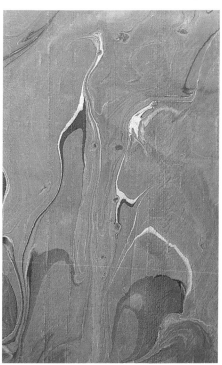

See also: ◆◆◆◆◆◆◆◆◆◆◆◆

EMBELLISHMENTS p 117
PRACTICALITIES p 125

◆◆◆◆◆◆◆◆◆◆◆◆◆◆◆◆◆◆

EMBROIDERED CUSHIONS

In addition to the embroidered cushions in this chapter, there are several constructed fabric techniques including reverse appliqué (cutting away layers of fabrics to reveal different colours beneath), a patchworked stars and stripes design in bright green and orange and blue, and appliqué using silk dupion. The embroidery techniques include a cross stitch cushion based on patchwork motifs worked in one colour to give a subtle effect, and a mellow needlepoint cushion inspired by a Gothic style tile. Finally, there are three somewhat unusual cushion-making techniques: crocheted sunflowers; rag rug dining room chair covers, and a pieced-felt matryoshka doll. Embroidery comes in many guises — I hope you will enjoy the resulting cushions.

Reverse appliqué cushions

Inspired by antique woven brocades with symmetrical patterns and sumptuous velvet designs as found in Renaissance paintings, this cushion is made using reverse appliqué. This involves cutting away layers of fabric to reveal more layers of different-coloured fabric below the surface.

(DESIGNER: LUCINDA GANDERTON)

MATERIALS & EQUIPMENT

fine pen

tracing paper

tissue paper

40 cm (16 in) silk squares in pink, yellow, and bronze

pins

cotton threads (white, green, brown, ochre)

sewing needle

embroidery scissors

sewing machine

iron and ironing board

2 × 51 cm (20 in) squares velvet (green)

2 m (2 yd) fringing (yellow)

45 cm (18 in) square cushion pad

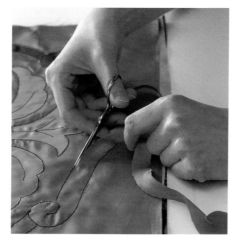

1 Using a photocopier, enlarge the design on page 76 to a suitable size and trace the pattern onto tissue paper. Pin the pink, yellow and bronze fabrics together and stitch the tracing to the reverse side of the bronze fabric. Machine stitching through all four layers in a straight outline stitch, work around the lines of the design.

2 Carefully remove the paper and turn the sewn fabric over so that the pink fabric is on top. With the sharp embroidery scissors, cut away one or two layers of fabric from parts of the design so that the different colours show through the top layer. Follow the finished cushion photograph opposite as a guide. Snip closely to the stitches.

OPPOSITE
The cut-away layers of silk on this cushion give it a textural, three-dimensional quality.

3 *Put the satin stitch foot onto your sewing machine and sew over the raw edges in satin stitch, tapering the stitches at the points. Change the cotton thread to an appropriate colour each time you work on a different part of the design.*

Reverse appliqué outline

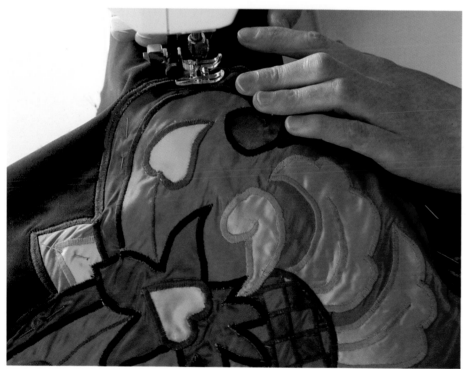

ABOVE
The reverse appliqué outline. Enlarge to an appropriate size (see step 1).

See also: ◆◆◆◆◆◆◆◆◆◆◆◆

GALLERY pp 40-1
EMBELLISHMENTS p 117
PRACTICALITIES p 125

◆◆◆◆◆◆◆◆◆◆◆◆◆◆◆◆◆◆

4 *Cut the excess fabrics from around the edge of the motif and press. Then pin the motif centrally to one of the velvet squares and use satin stitch to stitch it in place. With wrong sides facing, sew around three sides of the cushion cover, turn right sides out and insert the cushion pad. Slip-stitch the open side to close and sew fringing around the edge.*

RIGHT
Detail of the reverse
appliqué cushion. The
satin stitch gives a solid
edge that helps prevent
fraying when the
fabrics beneath are
cut away.

Crocheted cushions

Love of the sun, memories of long, languid holidays taken in the south of France and the work of Van Gogh all inspired the design for these charming and unusual sunflower-shaped cushions. They are crocheted from brightly-coloured cotton yarns.

(DESIGNER: RACHEL HOWARD MARSHALL)

Abbreviations
beg beginning; ch chain; dc double crochet (single crochet); htr half treble (half double crochet); sl slip; sl st(s) slip-stitch(es); tr treble (double crochet).

Front cushion
Using the size 4.00 crochet hook and orange yarn (main colour) work 3 ch. Join a ring with a sl st in first ch.
1st round 1 ch, 5 dc into ring, sl st in first dc at beg of round.
2nd round 1 ch, 2 dc in each of next 5 sts in first dc at beg of round.
3rd round 1 ch, 2 dc in each of next 10 sts, sl st in first dc at beg of round.
4th round Change to gold yarn (contrast). Work 1 ch, * 2 dc in first st, 1 dc in next st; rep from * 9 more times, sl st in first st at beg of round.
5th round Change to orange yarn. Work 1 ch, 1 dc in each of next 30 sts, sl st in first dc at beg of round.
6th round Change to gold yarn. Work 1 ch, * 1 dc in each of first 2 sts, 2 dc

OPPOSITE
Three golden sunflower cushions sitting in the autumn sun, their faces looking up for warmth.

in the next st; rep from * 9 more times, sl st in first st at beg of round.
7th round Change to orange yarn. Work 1 ch, * 1 dc in each of first 3 sts, 2 dc in next st; rep from * 9 more times, sl st in first st at beg of round.
8th round Change to gold yarn. Work 1 ch, 1 dc in each of next 50 sts, sl st in first dc at beg of round.
9th round Change to orange yarn. Work 1 ch, * 1 dc in each of first 4 sts, 2 dc in next st; rep from * 9 more times, sl st in first dc at beg of round.
10th round Change to gold yarn. Work 1 ch, * 1 dc in each of first 5 sts, 2 dc in next st; rep from * 9 more times, sl st in first dc at beg of round.
11th round Change to orange yarn. Work 1 ch, 1 dc in each of next 70 sts, sl st in first dc at beg of round.
12th round Change to gold yarn and work as for 11th round.
13th round Change to orange yarn and work as for 11th round.
14th round Change to gold yarn and work 1 ch, * 1 dc in each of first 6 sts, 2 dc in next st; rep from * 9 more times, sl st in first dc at beg of round.
15th round Change to orange yarn. Work 1 ch, 1 dc in each of next 80 sts, sl st in first dc at beg of round.

MATERIALS & EQUIPMENT

double-knit cotton yarn in the following colours:
40 g (1½ oz) orange (main colour)
20 g (¾ oz) gold (contrast)
40 g (1½ oz) yellow
50 g (2 oz) green

crochet hook (size 4.00)

scissors

tapestry needle

150-200 g (5-7 oz) cushion filling

16th round 1 ch, * 1 dc in each of first 7 sts, 2 dc in next st; rep from * 9 more times, sl st in first dc at beg of round.
17th round 1 ch, 1 dc in each of next 90 sts, sl st in first dc at beg of round.
18th round Work as for 17th round. Cast off. Sew in and trim all ends.

Petals (make 10 alike)
Using the size 4.00 crochet hook and yellow yarn, work as follows:
1st row 12 ch, 1 sl st in 2nd ch from hook, 1 sl st in next st, 1 dc in each of the next 3 sts, 1 htr in each of next 3 sts, 1 tr in each of the last 3 sts, 3 ch, turn.
2nd row 1 tr in each of first 3 sts, 1 htr in each of next 3 sts, 1 dc in each of next 3 sts. Working around the end of row and back along the previous row, work 1 sl st in each of next 5 sts, 1 dc in each of next 3 sts, 1 htr in each of 3 sts, 1 tr in each of last 3 sts, 3 ch, turn.

3rd row *1 tr in each of first 3 sts, 1 htr in each of next 3 sts, 1 dc in each of next 3 sts. Working around the tip of the petal, work 1 sl st in each of next 7 sts, 1 dc in each of next 3 sts, 1 htr in each of next 3 sts, 1 tr in each of last 3 sts. Cast off.*

Repeat rows 1-3, 9 more times. On the last petal do not cast off, join all the petals together as follows:

9 sl sts along the bottom edge of each petal to form a string of petals. Cast off leaving a yarn end measuring 150 cm (60 in). Thread a tapestry needle to the yarn end and overstitch the petals to the front of the cushion, stitching into the front loop of each stitch on the last row of the front cushion.

Back cushion

Using size 4.00 crochet hook and green yarn only, work as for front cushion, rounds 1-18. Keep the yarn attached to work the leaves.

Turn the back of the cushion around, so wrong side of work faces you, and work as follows:

19th round ** 7 ch, 1 sl st in 2nd ch*

from hook, 1 dc in next ch, 1 htr in next ch, 1 tr in next ch, 1 tr in each of last 2 chs. Join the leaf to the cushion back with a sl st in the 4th st from beg of 7 ch, 1 sl st in each of next 5 sts; rep from * 9 more times. Cast off, leaving a yarn end measuring 150 cm (60 in).

Making up the cushion

Thread a tapestry needle to the 150 cm (60 in) green yarn end. From the back of the cushion, position the leaves between the yellow petals. Over stitch the back cushion to the front, stitching into the back loop of each stitch on the last row of the front cushion. Leave a 7.5-10 cm (3-4 in) opening, pad the cushion with filling and sew up the opening.

RIGHT
The bright colours of
this sunflower cushion
brings a glow to the
onset of autumn.

LEFT
Detail of a sunflower
cushion showing the
crocheted chain stitches
that are used to make
the body of the cushion
and the petals.

See also: ◆◆◆◆
GALLERY p 21
RAG RUG CUSHIONS
    pp 100-03
PRACTICALITIES p 125
◆◆◆◆◆◆◆◆◆◆◆

Machine-embroidered cushions

This cushion is inspired by medieval decoration as reinterpreted by the Victorians for a gentleman's study. It has been richly upholstered in the traditional style, and the metallic organza and gold thread create a glistening and sumptuous cushion.

(DESIGNER: LUCINDA GANDERTON)

MATERIALS & EQUIPMENT
....

tracing paper

pencil

tissue paper

scissors

15 x 30 cm (6 x 12 in) metallic organza

15 cm (6 in) square velvet (red)

needle

cotton thread (black)

sewing machine (swing needle)

machine embroidery thread (gold)

45 x 85 cm (18 x 34 in) velvet (black)

40 cm (16 in) square cushion pad

1 Enlarge the design on page 84 on a photocopier to a 40 cm (16 in) square and trace it onto tissue paper. Cut out the central fleur-de-lys motif and also cut out the same size square from the organza and red velvet fabrics. Pin the fabrics together with the organza on top and baste the tracing to the reverse side of the velvet, stitching through all three layers.

2 Outline the pattern on the tissue paper using the sewing machine and a straight stitch. Carefully remove the tissue and turn the fabric over. Trim surplus organza from around the fleur-de-lys motif, cutting close to the outside edge of the stitching. Using the satin stitch foot on your sewing machine, satin stitch in gold over the raw edges.

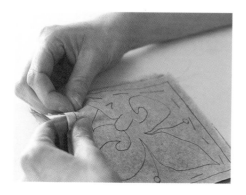

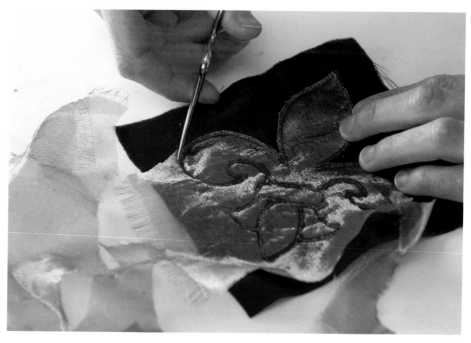

OPPOSITE
A mixture of machine embroidery and appliqué using luxurious fabrics are used to create an elegant cushion.

3 *Cut the black velvet into two 40 cm (16 in) squares and mark a 15 cm (6 in) diagonal square centrally on one piece of velvet. Stitch along the lines in gold satin stitch. Cut the remaining organza into four triangles using the triangle templates as a guide and baste one organza triangle along each side of the square.*

4 *Trace the triangle templates onto tissue paper and baste the tissue onto the reverse side of the velvet directly beneath the organza triangles. Outline the leaves and central veins on the back with straight stitch on the sewing machine, as before. Turn over and cut away the surplus organza.*

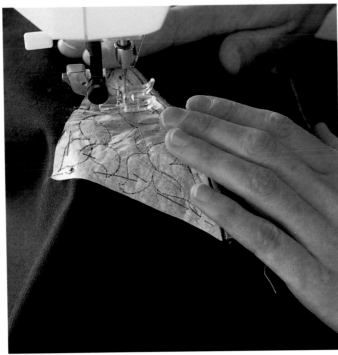

Stencil template

5   *Outline the branches and trunk with straight stitch on the reverse. Then on the right side, satin stitch in gold around the edges and the veins of the leaves and fill in the branches and trunk with free stitch using a darning foot. Sew the fleur-de-lys appliquéd motif into the centre with three rows of gold satin stitch.*

6   *With right sides facing, sew the two velvet squares together around three sides. Turn right sides out and insert the cushion pad. Fold under the raw edges and slip-stitch the open side together.*

See also: ◆◆◆◆◆◆◆◆◆◆◆◆◆

GALLERY pp 24, 35, 38, 39
EMBELLISHMENTS pp 114-15
PRACTICALITIES pp 120, 125

◆◆◆◆◆◆◆◆◆◆◆◆◆◆◆◆◆◆

OPPOSITE RIGHT
The appliqué and machine embroidery
outline. Enlarge to an appropriate size
(see step 1).

Cross stitch cushions

Here a traditional patchwork design has been translated into a design for cross stitch. The geometric shapes found in a patchwork design work just as well in cross stitch and the use of one colour makes for a very strong image. You might equally well work the design in another colourway or even using a number of colours.

(DESIGNER: ESTHER BURT)

MATERIALS & EQUIPMENT

....

graph paper (10 squares per in)

pencils

coloured pencils

ruler

11 count Aida evenweave fabric (cream)

cotton thread (contrast colour)

tapestry needle (size 26)

scissors

embroidery hoop

DMC stranded cotton thread (6 skeins of 321 red)

iron and ironing board

43 cm (17 in) square backing fabric

38 cm (15 in) square cushion pad

1 Draw your design (or copy the one given overleaf) onto graph paper. One square represents one cross stitch. It is best to draw your design in pencil initially so that you can rub out any mistakes as you go along. If you decide to use more than one colour, draw over the lines with coloured pencils to indicate what is going where.

2 Rule vertical and horizontal lines on the design to mark its centre. Find the centre of the canvas by folding it in half each way and running a line of large basting stitches in contrasting cotton thread to mark it. Then put the canvas into an embroidery hoop to hold it taut. Move the fabric along as you work each area of the design.

3 Starting at the centre of the canvas, embroider the design using three strands of the stranded cotton thread at a time and working the design in cross stitch. Remember that the top of each stitch should slant in the same direction as all the rest. Work from bottom left to top right.

4 When the design is finished, press it flat on the back. Allowing a 6 cm (2½ in) border around the cross stitch and a 12 mm (½ in) seam allowance, trim off the excess fabric. Cut a piece of backing fabric to the same dimensions and then make the cushion cover (see pages 121-3).

OPPOSITE
Cross stitch with style. The design of the cushion at the back is based on traditional quilt patterns, while the one in front is based on patchwork designs.

See also: ◆◆◆◆◆◆◆◆◆◆◆◆◆
NEEDLEPOINT CUSHIONS pp 90-91
PRACTICALITIES pp 120, 125
◆◆◆◆◆◆◆◆◆◆◆◆◆◆◆◆◆◆

OPPOSITE
Pattern for red
patchwork quilt cross
stitch cushion.

ABOVE
The red cross stitch cushion.
Start in the centre when
working your design.

Needlepoint cushions

The design on this cushion was inspired by a Gothic Revival floor tile designed for the Minton manufacturing company by Augustus Welby Pugin in the mid-19th century. The colours chosen are those of the period, but you can, of course, change the colour scheme to fit in with your decor.

(DESIGNER: LUCINDA GANDERTON)

MATERIALS & EQUIPMENT

25 cm (10 in) square single thread canvas (12 holes per in)

cotton thread

needle (fine)

tapestry needle

Appleton's tapestry yarns:
821 blue (3 skeins)
935 brown (5 skeins)
759 aubergine (2 skeins)
695 ochre (4 skeins)
692 cream (2 skeins)

plywood

buttonhole thread

iron and ironing board

20 cm (8 in) square velvet (toning shade)

polyester wadding

1 m (1 yd) cord (multicoloured)

See also: ◆◆◆◆◆◆◆◆◆◆◆◆◆

CROSS STITCH CUSHION pp 86-9
EMBELLISHMENTS pp 116-17
PRACTICALITIES pp 120, 125

◆◆◆◆◆◆◆◆◆◆◆◆◆◆◆◆◆

Needlepoint chart

Key

	821
	935
	759
	695
	692

1 Find the centre of the canvas by folding it in half each way and running a line of basting stitches in contrasting cotton thread to divide it into quarters.

2 Following the chart given to the right, work the design in tent stitch, starting with the centre cross motif and working outwards towards the edges. One square equals one stitch.

3 When completed, block the work to square it up by dampening it and then stretching over a piece of plywood cut to the same dimensions as the finished cushion. Pull the overlapping edges tightly across the back and hold in place with strong buttonhole thread, working side to side and up and down, and leave to dry. Remove from the board and press lightly on the back.

4 Trim down to a 20 cm (8 in) square, so that there is 12 mm (½ in) unused canvas all around the finished design. With right sides facing, baste to the velvet square, then sew around three sides. Turn right sides out and stuff firmly with the polyester wadding. Slip stitch the open side together and attach the cord to the outside edge, looping it at the corners.

Felt cushions

With her Czech background and love of all things Eastern European, Rachel Marshall has designed a cushion inspired by Russian matryoshka dolls. This pretty, shaped cushion is a fine example of folk art at its best. It is made completely from felt so there is no seam neatening to worry about.

(DESIGNER: RACHEL HOWARD-MARSHALL)

MATERIALS & EQUIPMENT

42 × 28 cm (17 × 11 in) black felt

pins

embroidery scissors

small pieces of felt (red, blue, green, pink, yellow, orange)

46 × 32 cm (18 × 13 in) white felt

needles

cotton threads (black, various colours)

pencil

pinking shears

46 × 32 cm (18 × 13 in) green felt

200-250 g (8-10 oz) toy filling

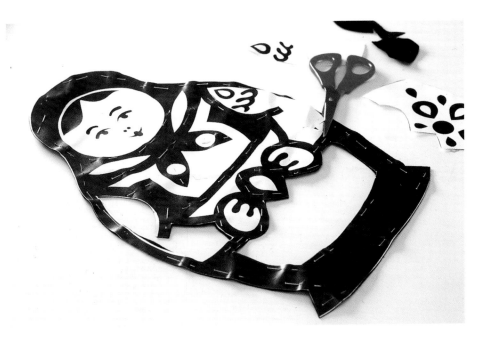

OPPOSITE
The matryoshka doll-shaped cushion worked in brightly coloured felts. Felts are so easy to stitch together.

RIGHT
The matryoshka doll template. Enlarge to an appropriate size (see step 1).

1 *Enlarge the doll template (right) on a photocopier to 40 × 26 cm (16 × 10 in). Pin the photocopy to the black felt and then cut out the doll starting from the outside and working in. Do not cut out the features or decorations from the black felt, instead cut them from the small pieces of coloured felts. Extra petals and shapes can be added to the design.*

Russian doll template

2 Place the black felt doll on the white felt and pin into place. Then stitch close to the edge of the black felt, either with a machine or by hand. Pin the features, hair and petals on the design and also stitch with matching sewing threads.

3 Mark a pencil line on the white felt 1.5 cm (⅝ in) from the outside edge of the black appliquéd doll. With pinking shears cut slightly inside the pencil line and then pin the appliquéd doll to the green felt. (This is to be the cushion back.) Using the pinking shears again, cut around the doll shape, 6 mm (¼ in) from the white felt edge.

4 On the white felt, stitch 1 cm (½ in) away from the black felt doll outline all the way around, leaving a 10 cm (4 in) opening at the base of the doll. Fill the cushion with the toy filling and stitch up the opening to finish.

See also: ◆◆◆◆◆◆◆◆◆◆◆◆

◆◆◆◆◆◆◆◆◆◆◆◆◆◆◆◆◆◆

RIGHT
Detail of the face and bodice on the cushion. Instead of sewing, it is easier to stick the finer details in place, such as the nostrils, mouth and eyebrows.

Patchwork and appliqué cushions

Amy Taylor has here designed a fun, appliqué cushion inspired by the symbolism of the American flag — the stars and stripes — in conjunction with the bright, cheerful colours found in contemporary nightclubs.

(DESIGNER: AMY TAYLOR)

OPPOSITE
A truly modern stars and stripes cushion made from bonded appliqué in contemporary colours.

MATERIALS & EQUIPMENT
....

0.5 m (½ yd) polycottons
(mid-blue, yellow, green, orange)

scissors

fusible webbing

iron and ironing board

20 cm (8 in) polycotton (pink)

tracing paper

sewing machine

cotton threads (pink, blue)

51 × 81 cm (20 × 31 in) backing fabric

46 cm (18 in) square cushion pad

1 Cut four 18 cm (7 in) mid-blue squares; one 18 cm (7 in) yellow square; and eight green and eight orange 5 × 18 cm (2 × 7 in) strips. Referring to the photograph opposite and using 6 mm (¼ in) seam allowances, sew four green and orange strips to either side of the yellow square (four strips should be the same size as the square). Make another two panels of pieced fabric by sewing the remaining green and orange strips together to make two squares and sew mid-blue squares to either side of them.

2 *Iron fusible webbing onto the back of the yellow and pink fabrics. Trace or photocopy the star template (right), cut it out and draw around it four times on the fusible webbing backing the yellow fabric, and once on the pink fabric backing.*

See also: ◆◆◆◆◆◆◆◆◆◆◆◆◆◆

GALLERY pp 19, 24, 33, 35, 39
EMBELLISHMENTS pp 114-15
PRACTICALITIES pp 120, 125
◆◆◆◆◆◆◆◆◆◆◆◆◆◆◆◆◆◆◆◆◆◆◆◆

ABOVE
Here is the star from the centre of the cushion. It has been positioned with fusible webbing and then the edges fastened in place with zigzag stitch.

*Star template
(actual size)*

3 Cut out the four yellow stars and the one pink one.

4 Peel the backing paper off the stars and iron the pink star into the centre of the yellow square and a yellow star into the centre of each blue square. Sew around the edge of each star with a close-set zigzag stitch to neaten and then sew the three panels together to form the cushion front. Make an envelope back with the backing fabric as described on page 121 and insert the cushion pad.

Rag rug cushions

A variety of materials and fabrics, including cotton, wool, nylon, jersey and felt, have been used in this cushion to produce a multi-textured surface. All recycled, they have been hooked through a hessian backing cloth. Depending on the desired effect, the fabrics can then either be left as loops, or they can be cut. It is worth planning your design first on some paper before transferring it onto the hessian backing.

(DESIGNER: LIZZIE REAKES)

OPPOSITE
Two church chairs with small hard seats made comfortable by the use of rag rug cushions worked in brightly coloured lively patterns.

1 Using the marker pen, sketch your design onto the hessian, allowing a 7.5 cm (3 in) border around the edge. Attach the hessian to the frame with either thumb tacks or by using a staple gun.

2 Cut the pieces of fabric for hooking. They should be cut along the straight of the grain and into strips about 1 cm (¾ in) wide. Begin hooking, starting from the centre and work outwards.

3 *Working with one hand under the frame, push the hook through the hessian. Guide the fabric strip over the hook to create a loop and then pull the loop back through the hessian, bringing the end of the strip to the top side. Push the hook through the hessian again, guide the fabric onto the hook and pull through to form a loop on the surface of the design. Repeat, remembering to always pull the fabric ends through to the top side.*

4 *Continue hooking, changing colours as desired and forming rows of loops, until a small area is filled. For a cut pile, at intervals, simply shear across the pile with a sharp pair of scissors.*

See also: ◆◆◆◆◆◆◆◆◆◆◆◆

GALLERY p 21
CROCHETED CUSHIONS pp 78-79
PRACTICALITIES p 125

◆◆◆◆◆◆◆◆◆◆◆◆◆◆◆◆◆◆◆

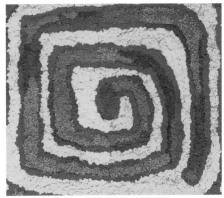

ABOVE
Detail of the finished cushion. Notice how different shades of blue have been used, giving the overall effect a charmingly patchy quality.

5 To finish the cushion, remove it from the frame and place face down on the floor. Spread a thin layer of latex all over the reverse side.

6 Cut around the shape leaving a 2.5 cm (1 in) border. After about 5 minutes fold in the border edges and leave to dry for at least 2 hours. Cut the ribbon into two and stitch both pieces by their centres to the back of the cushion using a strong, colour-coordinated thread. Protect the ribbon ties while applying a thin layer of latex onto the reverse and cover with calico or heavyweight muslin. To finish, apply latex to one side of the carpet webbing tape and position this around the border to avoid fraying. Allow to dry overnight before using.

103

Constructed fabric cushions

This cushion is made from pieces of material that have been sewn together to create the illusion of an intricately woven fabric. The secret of success when making this fabric is to be precise in all your measurements and cutting. The designer has used sumptuous slub silks in rich, jewel-like colours and applied them with machine embroidery threads. Her inspiration came from the colours of still-life compositions, including fruits, vegetables and rich fabrics. She puts them together and creates brocades, Regency stripes and damask.

(DESIGNER: CHARLOTTE HIRST)

MATERIALS & EQUIPMENT

2 pieces silk dupion (purple, pink)

cushion pad

scissors

fusible webbing

iron and ironing board

sewing machine

machine embroidery thread (pink, lime green)

tailor's chalk

velvet

cotton thread

OPPOSITE
Two jewel-like cushions made by first constructing the fabric and then the cushions.

1 *Cut the cushion front (purple silk dupion) so that it is the same size as the cushion pad plus 12 mm (½ in) seam allowances. Iron the fusible webbing onto the back of the contrast silk and cut the silk into 2 cm (¾ in) wide strips.*

2 *Peel the backing paper off the strips and place the silk strips on the front of the cushion cover so that they form evenly spaced lines. Iron these in place and then add the crosswise strips, so a grid is formed. Iron into place to secure them.*

3 Set your sewing machine to a
close zigzag stitch and use
machine embroidery thread to give a
sheen to the stitching. Stitch along
each side of the strips, covering the
raw edges as you sew.

4 Change to a green machine
embroidery thread. Mark the
centre of each check with a piece of
tailor's chalk. Using the embroidery
foot of the sewing machine, drop the
feed-dog and lower the foot onto the
fabric at the place where the spot is
marked. Make a small green spot. If
the fabric begins to pucker, remove it
and stretch it taut with the aid of an
embroidery hoop.

See also: ◆◆◆◆◆◆◆◆◆◆◆

GALLERY pp 33, 39
EMBELLISHMENTS pp 111-13
PRACTICALITIES pp 120, 125

◆◆◆◆◆◆◆◆◆◆◆◆◆◆◆◆

5 Make up the cushion by cutting the fabric for the back so that it is the same size as the front. With the right sides facing sew the front to the back of the cushion around three sides. Turn right sides out, insert the cushion pad and sew up the opening.

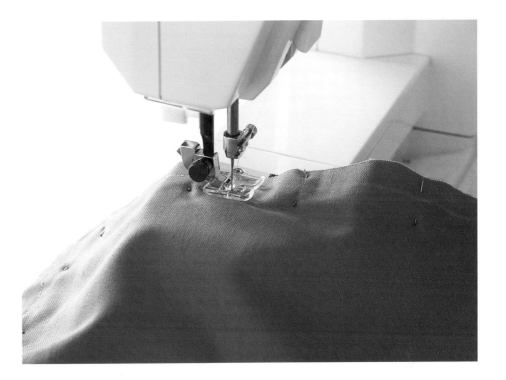

EMBELLISHMENTS AND FASTENINGS

*Cushions may be embellished or dressed up by the
addition of buttons, cord, braid or any other type
of trimming. The cushion does not need to be made
of a sumptuous or expensive material but may be
of very humble origins as are the three cushions
shown here. Made of calico, ticking, and gingham
in soft reds and blues, they are coordinated by the
clever use of colour, tone and texture — although
important, the decoration is kept to a minimum.
The cushion on the left has a lace trim, the one in
the centre has hand-made, fabric-covered buttons,
and the one on the right uses old-fashioned fabric
buttons with red running stitch. The appliquéd
cushion, above, has button trims used to add
colour, texture and movement to the design.*

(OPPOSITE LEFT: MELANIE WILLIAMS; OPPOSITE
CENTRE AND RIGHT: SARAH KING)

$\mathcal{B}$uttons and bows

As with clothes, cheap and nasty trims on a cushion will ruin the whole effect. It is worth trying to find the best trim you can, or to cover your own buttons. Old buttons may still be found, but make sure they are washable before laundering your precious cushion. Bows can be made from ribbon, grosgrain, the same fabric as the cushion cover, or a contrasting fabric. Buttons and bows can either be functional as closures or be purely decorative. A large bow in the centre of a cushion can make it seem like a present.

(DESIGNED BY MELANIE WILLIAMS UNLESS SPECIFIED OTHERWISE)

BELOW LEFT
Small real pearl buttons in a row are used to close this pretty blue cushion. The contrast in colour makes them a feature as well as a functional item.

BELOW
A number of different sized buttons were covered with coloured velvets and sewn all over the surface of this cushion as a form of interesting decoration.

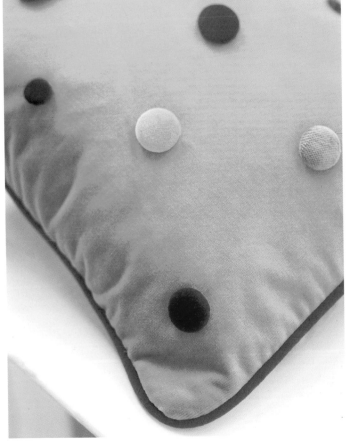

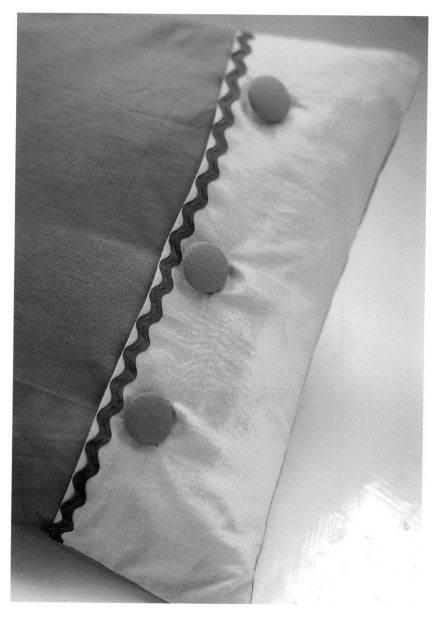

Tiny pearl buttons are the finishing touch on this cushion made from unbleached linen with a hand-edged centre panel of muslin. Note how the muslin is not sewn onto the cushion but instead is anchored by its corners with flat linen buttons.

ABOVE
Buttons hand-covered in three different colours turns what would be a useful closure into a decorative detail.

RIGHT
Simple ginghams, checks and even tea towel fabrics can be used to make cushion covers for the kitchen. This cushion has been finished with buttons hand-covered in ticking that contrasts with the main fabric.

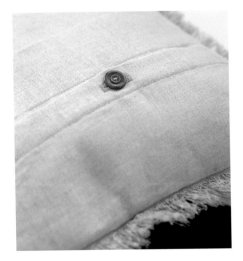

ABOVE LEFT
A colour story in blue is shown here. The flap and the hand-made ties of this cushion are in gingham and the body in blue check; a very good way of using up small pieces of fabric.

ABOVE
A pillowcase opening is reinforced with ties of grosgrain. The edges are cut at an angle to prevent fraying. There is enough grosgrain to tie in a knot but not a bow.

LEFT
A neat overlapping edge in satin stitch is used for the opening on this cushion. It has one button only and because it is large it needs a very neat buttonhole.

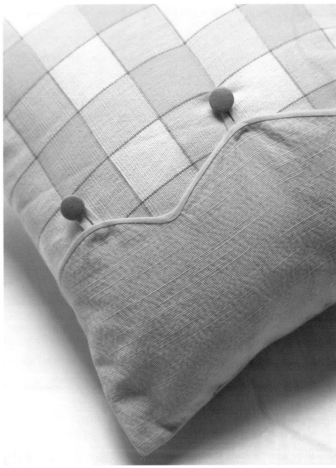

ABOVE

Small clusters of beads have been used to give a decorative finish to a very plain cushion. Tiny beads surround a slightly larger one. The edge of the cushion is decorated with a wavy band of white beads.

ABOVE RIGHT

A very pretty fastening is made by scalloping the edge of the flap on this cushion. It is bound in yellow bias and the loops too are made from the bias; the fastening is completed with contrasting self-covered buttons in blue.

RIGHT

The end of a bolster is covered by pulling up a drawstring so that it is tight and then tying it into a bow. The bolster ends are edged in a finely pleated frill.
(Damask)

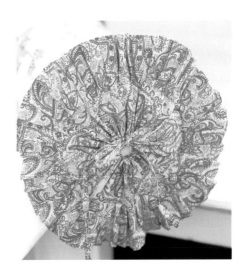

Appliqué

There are a number of different ways to embellish a cushion and, of those, appliqué can be the most imaginative. For example, by using old lace and pieces of ancient haberdashery, you can make a most pretty effect. The colours of the fabrics used will also affect the feel of the cushion. Create seasonal moods through the use of colour, such as autumnal browns and terracottas, or winter whites with contrasting reds, as found on holly berries. Use small-scale patterns for appliqués on small cushions. Ribbons may be used sewn in bands as on Eastern European folk costumes or even woven to create a chequerboard of colours.

BELOW
Pecking hens have been created by cutting semicircles from small-scale patterned fabrics. They have pearl button eyes, and their beaks and the flowers that they are eating are embroidered with simple stitches.

LEFT
Old lace has been used to edge this mauve cushion most effectively. At the overlapping corners, note how the bottom layer of lace is seen through the top layer.

ABOVE
Ribbon is woven to create a central panel.
This is done by pinning one end of each
piece of ribbon onto fusible webbing. The
pieces are woven and then the whole piece
is ironed onto the backing fabric.

RIGHT
An appliqué star has been made to
surround this buttonhole and a contrast
button added at the centre. This motif
could be repeated over the rest of the
cushion if desired.

Cords and tassels

The tassels and cords used to embellish a cushion are as important as the fabrics from which a cushion is made. A plain cushion may be made quite special by the use of an ornate cord edge, or a simple single or a more pronounced double piping. The corners of the cushion may be twisted, knotted or trimmed with tassels. These may be home-made (see page 125) or bought in haberdashery or soft furnishing departments. Cords and tassels do not have to be used on the edge of a cushion (see below right for a cording example); choose a cord that picks out the main colours or contrasts with the cushion design.

ABOVE
A plain cushion is edged with a piping that is inserted into the seams as the cushion is made. Piping has one flat edge specifically so that it may be sewn into the seams.

ABOVE
This small cushion is cleverly edged with a cord that is twisted at the corners. This size cushion would make an ideal ring cushion for a wedding.
(Lucinda Ganderton)

RIGHT
Cord is sewn in a spiral to create a decorative finish on this cushion. The stitching, or couching, is large and is part of the design. Use cord to make other shapes or to create a name or initials.

These cushions have all
been imaginatively
embellished with cords
and tassels. At the top
is a presentation
cushion in rich velvet
with a gold piped edge
and a gold tassel at
each corner. The
checked cushion has a
neat closure with a
piped edge and fabric-
covered buttons. The
chambray cushion has
elongated corners, long
enough to be tied into a
knot, and at the bottom
is an ikat woven fabric
finished with a fringe
worked in the same
colours. A very rich
damask needs a heavy
fringe such as this to
finish it off properly.
*(All by Cushions,
except second from top,
by Melanie Williams)*

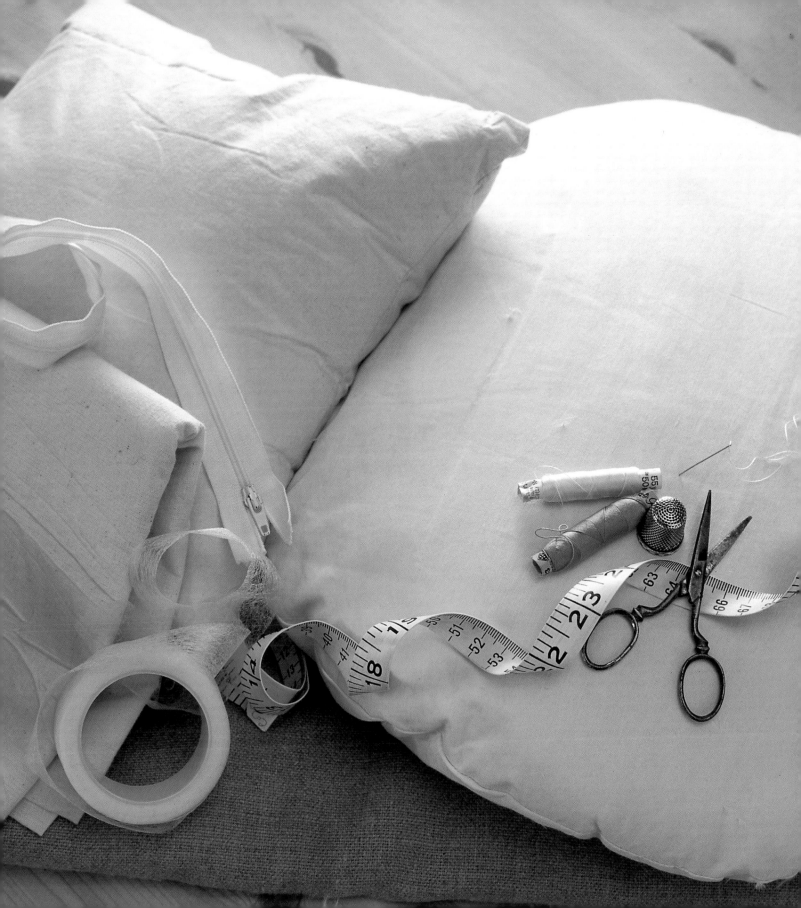

Practicalities

The wonderful thing about cushions is that as well as being an interesting area of interior detail and design, they also make life more comfortable. They add a hint of luxury and pampering to a room — the more you have, the cosier the room will be.

As well as being practical — whether used on a bed, sofa, out-doors, or even on the floor — and decorative in their own right, cushions can mask and distract the eye from a multitude of sins, from ageing chairs and sofas and uncomfortable seating. Few people can afford to rush out and buy new furniture every time someone spills coffee on the couch, or they get bored with the colour of their three-piece suite. New cushions are often a cheap and effective alternative.

Because an average-sized cushion doesn't use very much material, it is not normally a major expenditure. Having said this, I would warn against making covers with cheap fabric which is too flimsy or weak — the seams will be under too much pressure, and the fabric will soon tear. If you do want to cover cushions with very delicate fabrics, back the more delicate material with a stronger fabric, such as cotton.

Calculating the amount of material you need will really depend on the style of cushion you intend to make — one edged with a frill may use significantly more material than you expect, so estimate accurately before you buy or cut your fabric.

It is essential to bear in mind that you may need extra fabric if you have to make allowance for the direction of the pattern or the weave. Even a plain-coloured fabric such as velvet will not look as effective if the fabric does not match up — unless, of course, you are particularly looking for contrast.

If you are making the cushion pad, cover the filling with a sturdy fabric such as ticking, cambric, calico or heavyweight muslin. It is then possible to take the outer cover off to wash it — essential if you are using the cushion a lot. Fillings of pure down or down-and-feather mixes make soft, comfortable cushions which remain plump and won't lose their shape; in time, they may need to be replaced. Less expensive fillings include latex or plastic foam chips, but these aren't as luxurious and comfy, and won't keep their shape forever as they can become lumpy or disintegrate. You can also buy foam in slabs or blocks, ideal for garden seat cushions and sculpted shapes. They can be cut with a craft knife so that they fit the shape of your seat exactly.

For a professional finish to a cushion, a very useful (if slightly unusual) tip is to make the dimensions of the cover a little less than the size of the cushion pad. This way, the pad will fit more snugly, and the cover won't hang loosely, ruining the effect of plumpness and pertness which makes a cushion look fresh and appealing. Also, always remember to overstuff the cushion, or at the very least be generous with the stuffing, as it will soon settle and appear to have lost some of its original size.

Mixing styles and finishes

There are certain traditional styles of cushions which are widely used, and certain specific sewing tips and techniques which help to create these styles. However, these traditions are not carved in stone, and some of the most effective cushions are created by mixing and matching the different cushion types — and also sometimes by cheating and taking short cuts. For example, a mock Oxford, or self-bordered, cushion can be created simply by making a basic cover (leave the piping off for this) that is 5 cm (2 in) bigger all around than the cushion pad to be covered. When it has been finished and pressed, run either satin stitch or two lines of machine stitch a few millimetres apart around all four sides of the cushion 5 cm (2 in) from the edges.

You can also mix different styles: add a frill to a basic piped cushion; use piping to finish off a bolster; supplement cord for piping, or shape cushions into unusual fantasies such as stars and moons. Box cushions are great for the garden, though they can look very smart indoors, too.

Making piping

Piping cord is available in different thicknesses. Cotton cord must be shrunk before use, so boil it in clean water for 5 minutes and then dry thoroughly. Always cover the piping cord with fabric cut on the bias, unless the lines to be piped are straight, in which case this is not essential. When attaching two pieces of covering fabric, make sure to join them at an angle, on the straight of the grain, to avoid bunching.

To make piping cut strips of fabric to a width of 3.75 cm (1½ in). Lay the pre-shrunk cord along the centre of the strip, on the wrong side. Fold the fabric in half, with wrong sides facing, and pin. Using a zipper or piping foot on your sewing machine, stitch the piping snugly into the fabric. You will now have a piece of covered piping, with two seams free, that can be sewn into the cushion cover as required.

Cut bias strips

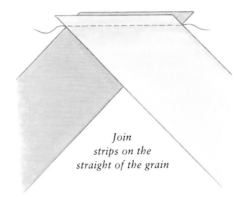

Join strips on the straight of the grain

Piped cushion

MATERIALS & EQUIPMENT

chosen fabric

scissors

cushion pad

pins

piping (or cord)

needle

cotton thread

zip

sewing machine

iron and ironing board

Calculations

Front Cut one piece of fabric the size of your cushion pad plus 15 mm (⅝ in) seam allowances.
Back To accommodate the zip, cut two pieces for the back — one large and one small. On the larger piece, allow 2 cm (¾ in) seam allowance on the lower edge for the zip, and 15 mm (⅝ in) seam allowances on the other three sides. For the smaller piece, cut a strip that is 5 cm (2 in) wide, plus the 15 mm (⅝ in) seam allowances and 2 cm (¾ in) zip allowance.

How to make

1 Make the piping (see left). With right sides facing, place the front and two back pieces together and notch all sides.

2 On the front piece, pin the piping all around the edge of the fabric on the seam allowance, stopping 15 mm (⅝ in) from each corner. At each corner, snip up to the piping stitching line, then stitch the piping in place so that the cut is at a 90-degree angle, and the corner is square. Join the ends of the piping.

3 Stitch the zip between the two back pieces.

4 With right sides facing, match up the notches, and then pin the back of the cushion to the front. Pin along the seam line at right angles.

5 Leaving the pins in position, machine stitch all the way around as close to the piping stitching line as possible. Remove the pins, turn right sides out and check that the previous stitching is not visible (if it is, re-stitch inside the last line). Turn inside out again and trim the corners to within 3 mm (⅛ in) of the stitching line, and then secure by stitching across the corners. Turn right sides out. Push the corners out with scissors or a pencil, press, and insert the cushion pad.

Round piped cushion

MATERIALS & EQUIPMENT

chosen fabric

scissors

circular cushion pad

paper

iron and ironing board

zip

pins

piping

needle

cotton thread

sewing machine

Calculations

Front Cut one piece of fabric to the diameter of the cushion pad adding a 1 cm (⅜ in) seam allowance all around.

Back Cut a piece of paper to the same size as the front fabric, cut in half and pin the two halves on the fabric 3 cm (1¼ in) apart.

How to make

1 To put in the zip, cut the oval in two across the shorter measure. With right sides facing, place the two pieces together, pin along the zip seam and baste together 15 mm (⅝ in) from the edge. Remove the pins, mark a central gap the size of the zip, and machine stitch along the seam leaving a gap for the zip where marked. Press the seams open and insert the zip.

2 Make enough piping (see page 120) to go around the circumference of the cushion plus 2.5 cm (1 in). Attach to the front cover piece (see Piped Cushion on page 120) and join the ends of the piping.

3 With right sides facing, place the front and back pieces together, and pin around the edge (making sure the zip is partly open). Baste around the edge and remove the pins.

4 Machine stitch all around, following the piping basting stitches around the edge.

5 Trim the seam, and snip out 'V's at regular intervals around the entire circle, making sure not to cut into the hem stitching. Turn right sides out and press.

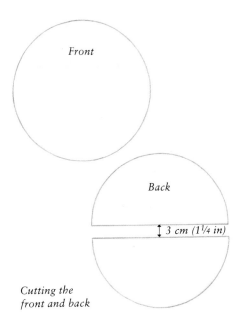

Front

Back

↕ 3 cm (1¼ in)

Cutting the
front and back

Envelope-back cushion

MATERIALS & EQUIPMENT

chosen fabric

scissors

cushion pad

sewing machine

cotton thread

pins, needle

iron and ironing board

Calculations

Front Cut one piece of fabric the size of your cushion pad plus 3 cm (1¼ in) seam allowances.

Back Cut two pieces of fabric, both the same width as the front, but half the length plus 15.5 cm (6¼ in).

How to make

1 To prepare the back, machine stitch a hem 2.5 cm (1 in) along the side of each piece of fabric that will eventually be overlapping.

2 Baste the two back pieces together, overlapping the hemmed edges by 10 cm (4 in). Once basted together, they should measure the same, both in length and depth, as the piece of fabric which has been cut out for the front.

3 Pin the front and back together, right sides facing. Baste, then machine sew, leaving 3 cm (1¼ in) seam allowance.

4 Trim the seams and turn right sides out. Push the corners out with scissors or a pencil, and press. Remove the basting and insert the cushion pad.

Oxford-style (self-bordered) cushion

MATERIALS & EQUIPMENT

chosen fabric

scissors

cushion pad

pins

zip

iron and ironing board

sewing machine

Calculations

Front Cut one piece of fabric the size of your cushion pad, adding 25 cm (10 in) to the dimensions.
Back Cut one piece of fabric the same width as the front, but measuring 5 cm (2 in) longer to allow for the zip.

How to make

1 Cut a strip 14 cm (5½ in) wide from the back length, and then pin it back in the same place, making a 2.5 cm (1 in) seam allowance for the zip. Stitch 14 cm (5½ in) in from each side. Press, and then insert the zip.

2 Place both the front and back pieces right sides down on your worksurface. Working each side consecutively, fold in 7 cm (2¾ in) and press. Fold the corners under, and pin in place.

3 Place front and back pieces together with wrong sides facing. Line up, making sure that the corners lie flat and meet each other with the corners folded in opposite directions. Pin around all four sides, 5 cm (2 in) from the edge.

4 Satin stitch around all four sides, following the pins. Remove the pins and insert the cushion pad.

Box cushion

MATERIALS & EQUIPMENT

chosen fabric

scissors

cushion pad

zip (width of cushion plus 15 cm / 6 in)

sewing machine

cotton thread

pins

iron and ironing board

piping

Calculations

Top and bottom Cut two pieces of fabric the size of your cushion pad plus 4 cm (1½ in) seam allowances.

Front gusset Cut one piece of fabric measuring the width and depth of the pad, adding 4 cm (1½ in) to both measurements.
Side gussets Cut two pieces of fabric measuring the length and deducting 4.5 cm (1¾ in); and measuring the depth and adding 3 cm (1¼ in).
Back gusset Cut one piece of fabric measuring the width and adding 18 cm (7 in); and measuring the depth and adding 6 cm (2½ in).

How to make

1 Cut the back gusset piece in half lengthwise, and insert the zip.

2 Pin the gusset pieces together making 15 mm (⅝ in) seam allowances and check that the complete gusset fits around the cushion pad neatly. Make alterations if necessary. Baste along the pinned seams and remove pins. Machine stitch, then press seams open.

3 Apply piping around the top and bottom pieces of fabric (see Piped Cushion on page 120). Snip the corners of the piping skirt.

4 With right sides facing, pin the gusset to the top piece all around. Baste along the line of piping, remove the pins and machine very close to basting.

5 Attach the bottom piece of fabric to the gusset in the same way, making sure that the zip is partly open while this is done.

Squab cushion

MATERIALS & EQUIPMENT

newspaper

masking tape

pencil

scissors

foam pad

polyester wadding

lining fabric

chosen fabric

fabric for ties (same or
contrasting fabric)

pins

sewing machine

cotton thread

piping

iron and ironing board

buttons (optional)

needle (optional)

upholstery thread (optional)

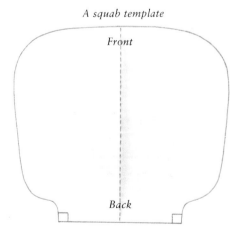

A squab template

Front

Back

Calculations

Template Make an accurate template
of the chair seat. To do this secure a
sheet of newspaper over each side
with masking tape. Fold the paper
back on itself around the back and
legs of the chair, mark the seat line
with a pencil, and then cut around the
leg to the side of the seat. Mark other
sides with a pencil. Remove
newspaper and cut to shape.
Foam pad Cut to shape of template.
Wadding Cut two pieces; one to fit the
pad, the other slightly larger.
Lining Cut two pieces to the same
shape as the pad, but add half the side
depth plus 15 mm (⅝ in) seam
allowances all around.
Main fabric Cut two pieces of fabric
to the same shape as the pad adding
2.5 cm (1 in) seam allowances.

How to make

1 Place the smaller piece of
wadding on top of the pad and
then place the pad on the other piece
of wadding. Fold the excess wadding
up over sides to meet the top piece,
feathering it out until it sticks to itself.

2 Make up four ties and enough
piping to go around the cushion
(see page 120).

3 Pin the pieces of lining fabric
together with right sides facing,
and stitch around three sides
(including the leg cut-outs), making
15 mm (⅝ in) seam allowances. Turn
right sides out, insert the foam pad,
and slip stitch along the back to close.

4 Pin the piping all around the top
piece of the main fabric as
described in the Piped Cushion on
page 120. The piping will lie flat if
you carefully snip it into curves and
leg cut-outs.

5 With right sides facing, pin, baste
and stitch the top piece to the
bottom piece for 3 cm (1¼ in) along
the back at each side. Stitch the zip in
place, and stitch the ties onto both
sides of each leg cut-out.

6 Pin the top piece to the bottom
piece all the way around along
the seam allowance, pinning to the
piping stitching line (make sure the zip
is undone slightly when you do this).
Stitch together, turn right sides out
and press.

7 If using buttons, put the cover on
the pad and mark the button
positions on either side of the cushion.
Sew on the buttons through the pad
from the bottom to the top, using a
sturdy needle and upholstery or other
strong cotton thread, knotting to
finish and secure.

Tied bolster cushion

This bolster cushion is actually very
simple to make because it only
involves working with one main piece
of fabric. For different finished effects,
gather the fabric at the ends of the
bolster by sewing on a button, tassel
or rosette.

MATERIALS & EQUIPMENT

chosen fabric

scissors

bolster pad

iron and ironing board

pins

sewing machine

cotton thread

Calculations

Cover Cut one piece of fabric which measures the length of the bolster pad plus the diameter of one end plus 6 cm (2½ in); the width of the fabric should measure the circumference of the bolster plus 6 cm (2½ in).
Ties Cut two strips of fabric 4 cm (1⅝ in) wide by the length of the main fabric.

How to make

1 Pin the long edges of the cover together with right sides facing; machine stitch, making a 15 mm (⅝ in) seam allowance. Press the seam open and turn right sides out.

2 Turn 1 cm (⅜ in) of fabric in at each end, pin and press.

3 Make a double hem by turning a further 2 cm (¾ in) of fabric inwards at each end, then pin and machine stitch. Make up the fabric ties.

4 Unpick the seam stitches where they overlap with the double hems at each end of the cover. Feed a fabric tie around each end by attaching a safety pin to the end of each tie.

5 Insert the bolster pad and make sure it is central. Then pull the fabric ties to gather the ends and neaten by tying into bows.

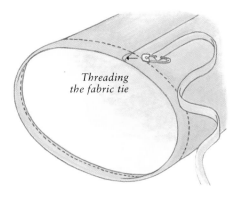

Threading the fabric tie

Heart-shaped cushion

MATERIALS & EQUIPMENT

paper

scissors

cotton fabric (not too thick)

pins

sewing machine

cotton thread

polyester filling

needle

lace/broderie anglaise (eyelet) trim (optional)

iron and ironing board

chosen fabric

snap fasteners

Calculations

Template Decide on the size and shape of the heart and cut a pattern out of paper.
Cotton fabric Cut out two pieces the same size as the template adding 1 cm (⅜ in) seam allowance all around.
Main fabric Cut one piece the same size as the cotton fabric (the front). For the back, cut the heart template in two (see diagram) and position on the fabric leaving a gap of 7.5 cm (3 in) for the fastening.

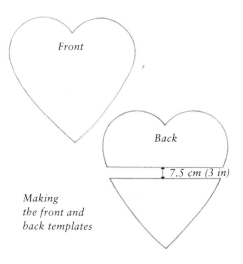

Front

Back

7.5 cm (3 in)

Making the front and back templates

How to make

1 Make the cushion pad by pinning and basting the two pieces of cotton fabric together, with right sides facing. Remove the pins and machine stitch 1 cm (⅜ in) from the edges all the way around, but leaving an opening of around 4 cm (10 in) on one side. Trim the seam, snip out 'V's, turn right sides out and fill with polyester. Slip stitch the gap to close.

2 To prepare the frill, join the ends of the lace/broderie anglaise (eyelet) trim together with a narrow seam. Finish off the seam with zigzag stitch, and press to one side. Mark the halfway point of the lace from the seam and gather the frill along the hem edge. Break off the threads at the two halfway points.

Pinning the frill to the front

3 Pin the frill onto the front piece of the main fabric, with right sides facing and the frill seam at the top of the heart. Make sure the gathers are even and pointing towards the middle of the cushion, and then baste and machine stitch, leaving a 12 mm (½ in) seam allowance. Baste the outer edges of lace onto the right side of the front.

4 Complete the back section of the heart cover by folding 2.5 cm (1 in) of each of the two parts of fabric back on themselves. Press, and secure the edges with zigzag stitch.

5 Overlap the two halves of the back by 2.5 cm (1 in), and stitch 5 cm (2 in) in from each side (this will vary depending on the size of the cushion). Sew on snap fasteners.

6 Pin the back of the heart cover onto the front, right sides facing. Baste together and remove the pins, then, with the front of the cover on top, machine stitch, following the frill stitching line.

7 Trim the seam, snipping out 'V's around curves and in the heart dip. Turn right sides out and finish off by removing the basting on the lace/broderie anglaise (eyelet) and press.

Making tassels

Wind yarn around two pieces of card placed together. The width of the card should be the length of the finished tassel. While the yarn is still on the card, insert a length of yarn through the top of the tassel and tie it firmly together. Then thread another piece of yarn through this loop several times (this will later be used for attaching the tassel). Cut the other ends of the yarn, remove the card, and bind the tassel 12 mm (½ in) from the top of the uncut side.

Tieing the top of the tassel

Binding the tassel

cut

Care of cushions

It almost goes without saying that cushions which are to be used in a kitchen — where they are likely to become affected by heat, steam and condensation as a result of cooking and washing and the hurly-burly of family life — must have easily removable covers that can be laundered easily. Make sure these covers are made of pre-shrunk fabrics.

For cushions which are to be used outdoors, fabrics need to be chosen with equal care. They should be hard-wearing, stain-resistant and as snag-proof as possible if they are to be used on the ground or stay outside. They also need to be damp- and rot-proof. One way to overcome the problem of damp is to make a cushion with a plastic-covered pad and a towelling cover, which is soft but can be removed and washed with ease.

The feathers or foam of the cushion should be encased in an inner cover made from lining fabric, so that the innards remain intact when the cover is removed for washing.

When making your own covers, check that both the cover and trims (including embellishments) are suitable for washing. Any cushion with antique or valuable embellishments should be taken to a specialist cleaner. Old buttons where the dye quality is in doubt should be removed before laundering.

Bibliography

Embroidered Church Kneelers by Barbara Thomson and Wendy Trewin, published by Batsford (1987)

Make Your Own Cushions and Covers and *Make Your Own Curtains and Blinds* by Lani van Reenen, published by New Holland (Publishers) Ltd (1993)

Pin Cushions by Avril Colby, published by Batsford (1975 and 1988)

Seventeenth-century Interior Decoration in England, France and Holland by Peter Thornton, published by Yale University (1990)

The Complete Upholsterer by Carole Thomerson, published by Frances Lincoln (1989)

The Soft Furnishing Book by Katrin Cargill, published by Mitchell Beazley (1994)

The Victoria and Albert Museum's Textile Collection 1200 to 1750, published by the Victoria and Albert Museum (1993)

Contributors and stockists

CONTRIBUTORS

Roz Arno (textile artist)
"Highbury"
Post Office Lane
Cleeve Hill
Nr Cheltenham
GL52 3PS
Tel: 01242 673174

Helen Banzhaf (machine embroideries)
31 Lampmead Road
Lee
London SE12 8QJ
Tel: 0181 852 9672

Esther Burt
c/o the author

Bentley and Spens
90 Lots Road
London SW10 0DQ
Tel: 0171 352 5685

Bery Designs
157 St Johns Hill
London SW11 1TQ

Sarah Collins
Home Farm
Delaport
Lamer Lane
Wheathampstead
Herts AL4 8RQ
Tel: 01582 833483

Clare Cox (textile design)
Waterside
99 Rotherhithe Street
London SE16 4NF
Tel: 0171 231 9049
Fax: 0171 231 9051

Cushions, Unit 6
98 Victoria Road
London NW10 6NB
Tel: 0181 963 0994
Fax: 0181 961 0430

Damask
Unit 7, Mail order dept
Sulivan Enterprise Centre
Sulivan Road
London SW6 3DJ

Dawn Dupree
6 Grove Vale
East Dulwich
London SE22 8EF
Tel: 0171 738 6720

Anna French Ltd
343 King's Road
London SW3 5ES
Telephone: 0171 351 1126

Lucinda Ganderton
23 Albany Passage
Richmond
Surrey, TW10 6DL
Tel: 0181 940 7617

Hampshire and Dillon (contemporary home accessories)
34 Seaton Point
London E5 8PY
Tel: 0181 533 1379

Charlotte Hirst (textile designer)
c/o 30 Church St
Bishop Middlehoun
County Durham
DL17 9AS

Peter Keay
18B Vicarage Gate
Kensington
London W8 4AA
Tel: 0171 937 3836

Sarah King
Waterside
99 Rotherhithe Street
London SE16 4NF

Sally Mansfield-Carter
The Mulberry Tree
120 Hydethorpe Road
Clapham South
London SW12 0JD
Tel: 0181 675 5164
Fax: 0181 675 5164

Rachel Marshall
111 Dunstan's Road
East Dulwich
London SE22 0HD
Tel: 0181 693 0775

Carole McCue
45 The Rock, Helsby
Cheshire WA6 9AS
Tel: 01928 724488

Rachel McDonnell
Unit 11
Chaucer Court
Workshops
Chaucer Street
Nottingham NG1 5LP
Tel: 0115 584207

Kim Meyer Designs
Studio 6
Cockpit Workshops
Northington Street
London WC1N 2NP
Tel: 01850 612126
Fax: 0171 916 2455

Bettina Mitchell
South Bank Craft Centre
Royal Festival Hall
South Bank
London SE1

Lorna Moffat
38 Cannon Woods Way
Kennington
Ashford
Kent TN24 9QY
Tel: 01233 638508

Liz Mundle (fibre artist)
401.5 Workshops
401.5 Wandsworth Road
London SW8 2JP
Tel: 0171 622 7261
Ansaphn: 0181 673 0156

Sarbjit Natt
20 Elms Avenue
London N10 2JP
Tel: 0181 883 4503

Trisha Needham
Clockwork Studios
38B Southwell Road
London SE5 9PG

Hikaru Noguchi
Unit W4 Cockpit
Workshops
Cockpit Yard
Northington St
London WC1N 2NP
Tel: 0171 916 3823

Lizzie Reakes
68 Oaklands Road
Hanwell, Ealing
London W7
Tel: 0181 840 7579

Cyndy Shear
44 Goldsmith Avenue
Acton
London W3
Tel: 0181 992 1566

Lisa Skelton
Unit 51 Penny Bank
Chambers
33-35 St Johns Square
London EC1M 4DS

Zara Siddiqui
Tel/Fax:
   0181 851 1471

Jillian Stewart
136 Holland Street
Glasgow G2 4NB

Amy Taylor
420 Leymour Road
Golcar
Huddersfield
West Yorkshire HD7 4QF
Tel: 01484 655131

Alison Tilley
c/o 40 Parkland Road
Woodford Green
Essex IG8 9AP
Tel: 0181 504 0326

Suzanne White
1 Hollybrook Cottage
Woodhouses, Yoxall
Burton-upon-Trent
Staffordshire DE13 8NR
Tel: 01543 472861
Fax: 01543 472810

Melanie Williams
45b Lansdowne Drive
Hackney
London E8
Tel: 0171 254 0012

Lisa Vaughan
Unit 228, Highbury
Workshops
Aberdeen House
22 Highbury Grove
London N5 2EA

STOCKISTS

Bery Designs
157 St Johns Hill
London SW11 1TQ

Damask
Unit 7, Mail order dept
Sulivan Enterprise Centre
Sulivan Road
London SW6 3DJ

Dawn Dupree
6 Grove Vale
East Dulwich
London SE22 8EF
Tel: 0171 738 6720

Anna French Ltd
343 King's Road
London SW3 5ES
Telephone: 0171 351 1126

Hampshire and Dillon
(contemporary home
accessories)
34 Seaton Point
London E5 8PY
Tel: 0181 533 1379

Hays Colours Ltd
55/57 Glengall Road
London SE15 6NQ

Sally Mansfield-Carter
The Mulberry Tree
120 Hydethorpe Road
Clapham South
London SW12 0JD
Tel: 0181 675 5164
Fax: 0181 675 5164

VV Rouleaux (ribbons,
trimmings and braids)
201 New King's Road
London SW6
Tel: 0171 371 5929
Fax: 0171 736 9065

George Weil and Sons Ltd
18 Hanson Street
London W1P 7DB
Tel: 0171 580 3763

USEFUL ADRESSES

United Kingdom

Cushions
8 Impress House
Vale Grove
London W3 7QP
(Retail/wholesale/fabrics)
(0181) 932 8788

Heal's
Tottenham Court Road
London W1P 9LD
(0171) 636 1666

John Lewis Partnership
278-306 Oxford Street
London W1A 6AH
(0171) 629 7711

Liberty Retail Ltd
210-220 Regent Street
London W1R 6AH
(0171) 734 1234

Arthur Sanderson & Sons
6 Cavendish Square
London W1M 9HA
(0171) 636 7800

Michael J Bracey
35-37 Alma Vale Road
Clifton
Bristol B58 2HS
(Fabrics/interior design)
(0117 9) 734 664

Roomours Design Ltd
28-32 Winchcombe Street
Cheltenham
Glos GL52 2LY
(Fabrics/furnishings)
(01242) 52 1155

Australia

Boronia Fabrics Pty Ltd
14 Campbell Street
Blacktown NSW 2148
(02) 671 3737

Burwood Craft Centre
173 Burwood Road
Burwood NSW 2134
(02) 747 5714

Bargain Upholstery
Fabrics
13 Burnt Road
Seaforth NSW 2093
(02) 948 2996

Parafield Soft Furnishings
and Fabrics
13 Research Road
Pooraka South Australia
5095
(08) 262 5984

Gwen's Timeless Crafts
133 Unley Road
Unley South Australia
5061
(08) 373 5271

Sundale Handcrafts
Shop 11 Logan
Hyperdome
Pacific Highway
Loganhome Queensland
4129
(07) 801 1121

In-Material Fabric Shoppe
Unit 2/135 Brown's Plain
Road
Brown's Plain
Queensland 4118
(07) 800 4025

Bargain Box Fabrics
352 South Street
O'Connor Western
Australia 6076
(09) 314 1359

New Zealand

Cushla's Village Fabrics
26 Victoria Road
Devonport
(09) 445 9995

Elna & Lincoln Fabrics
1017 Dominion Road
Mt Roskill
(09) 620 4954

Fabric Barn
13A The Concourse
Henderson
(09) 836 9071

Lighting Cutting Services
100 Honan Place
Avondale
 (09) 828 4686

Petes Fabrics
Karangahape Road
Auckland
(09) 358 0891

Fabric Closet
6 Bute Road
Browns Bay
(09) 478 7168

South Africa

Alladins Cave
West Side Centre
1 West Street
Kempton Park 1619
(011) 975 3120 and
(011) 823 4589

The Wool and Baby
Centre
208 Commercial Road
Pietermaritzberg 3201

Pied Piper
13 Kemfley Street
Emerald Hill
Port Elizabeth 6011
(041) 52 3090

Dot's Wool and
Handicraft
2 Hatfield Plaza
1131 Park Street
Hatfield
Pretoria 0083
(012) 43 2455

Petit Point Wool and
Handicrafts
Tyger Valley Centre
Willie van Schoor Avenue
Bellville 7530
(021) 948 2335

Style Fabrics
Shop S 206
South Mall
Oriental Plaza
Johannesburg 2001
(Mail order service)
(011) 836 0568

Kalicoscope
Zuby Paruk
119 Jan Hofmeyer Road
Durban 4091
(031) 2660253

Zhaun's
Dumbarton House
Adderley Street
Cape Town
(021) 230571

Index